Motorcycling in the

50s

3ol

To Eric Brockway, who played a prominent role in the British motorcycle industry during the period covered by this book. Although he willingly helped check the copy and provided photographs, sadly, he did not live long enough to see this book published.

Other books of interest to enthusiasts available from Veloce -

Alfa Romeo Owner's Bible
by Pat Braden
Alfa Romeo Modello 8C 2300
by Angela Cherrett
Alfa Romeo Giulia Coupe GT & GTA
by John Tipler
Biggles!
by Peter Berresford Ellis & Jennifer Schofield
Bubblecars & Microcars Colour Family Album
by Andrea & David Sparrow
Big Bugattis - Types 46 & 50
by Barrie Price
Bugatti 57 - The Last French Bugatti
by Barrie Price
Car Bodywork & Interior: Care & Repair
by David Pollard
Citroen 2CV Colour Family Album
by Andrea & David Sparrow
Citroen DS Colour Family Album
by Andrea & David Sparrow
Cobra: The Real Thing!
by Trevor Legate
Completely Morgan: Four-Wheelers 1936-1968
by Ken Hill

Completely Morgan: Four-Wheelers from 1968
by Ken Hill
Daimler SP250 'Dart'
by Brian Long
Fiat & Abarth 124 Spider & Coupe
by John Tipler
Fiat & Abarth 500 & 600
by Malcolm Bobbitt
How to give your MGB V8 Power
by Roger Williams
How to Power Tune Alfa Romeo Twin Cam Engines
by Jim Kartalamakis
Lola T70
by John Starkey
Mazda MX5/Miata Enthusiast's Workshop Manual
by Rod Grainger & Pete Shoemark
Mini Cooper: The Real Thing!
by John Tipler
Nuvolari: When Nuvolari Raced
by Valerio Moretti
Pass the MoT
by David Pollard
Rover P4 Series (60•75•80•90•95•100•105•110)
by Malcolm Bobbitt
Total Tuning for the Classic MG Midget/A-H Sprite
by Daniel Stapleton

First published in 1995 by Veloce Publishing Plc., Godmanstone, Dorset DT2 7AE, England. Fax 01300 341065

ISBN 1 874105 46 4

Readers with ideas for automotive books, or books on other transport or related hobby subjects are invited to write to the editorial director of Veloce Publishing at the above address.

British Library Cataloguing in Publication Data -
A catalogue record for this book is available from the British Library.

Typesetting (Suotane), design and page make-up all by Veloce on Apple Mac.

Printed and bound in England.

Motorcycling in the 50s

Jeff Clew

VELOCE PUBLISHING PLC
PUBLISHERS OF FINE AUTOMOTIVE BOOKS

Acknowledgements & Introduction

One of the nice things about writing a book is the way in which everyone responds when help is needed. I am grateful to a large number of good folk in this respect and, in mentioning them below, I hope I have not inadvertently missed anyone out.

Firstly, my sincere thanks to Allan Robinson M.B.E., who responded with characteristic cheerfulness when I asked him if he would read through the complete manuscript. He applied himself to this task with such dedication that his constructive criticism and many useful additions will, I hope, have made this a more readable and entertaining book. His mini cartoons that accompanied points he wished to emphasise raised a smile and helped make amending the text a less arduous task.

My good friend Eric Brockway very kindly checked the chapter on scooters, which led to some entertaining exchange of correspondence between us about the effect on stability of small diameter wheels. Ralph Venables, the doyen of motorcycling journalists, checked the chapter on how the two-stroke began to show its teeth in competitions, and provided the Christian names of most of the riders where I had only initials. Bob Cordon Champ provided some useful background information on the prototype Rainbow moped and its successor, the VeloSolex and the Swallow Gadabout.

Titch Allen B.E.M., Cyril Ayton, Norman Bown, Eric Brockway, Tony Brown, Castrol (U.K.) Ltd., Bob Cordon-Champ, Esso UK plc, Ken Harman, Joyce Miller, Nick Nicholls, Bruce Preston, Allan Robinson M.B.E., and the Royal Automobile Club all provided photographs and/or illustrations and kindly gave permission for them to be reproduced.

Period advertisements are very much part of a book like this and, in this respect, I would like to thank each of the following for giving me permission to reproduce those that have their copyright: J. Barbour and Sons Ltd., Castrol (U.K.) Ltd., Craven Equipment, Esso UK plc, Feridax (1957) Ltd., Goodyear Great Britain Ltd., Lucas Industries plc., Matchless Motorcycles Ltd., Norton

4

Motors (1993) Ltd., Phoenix Distribution (NW) Ltd. and Triumph Motorcycles Ltd. Some companies are no longer in business or have proved untraceable, so if I have inadvertently transgressed their copyright, I can only offer my apologies.

Last, but certainly not least, I would like to thank Rod Grainger and Judith St Claire-Pedroza, former colleagues from the Haynes Publishing Group, for having faith in my manuscript and making it the first motorcycling title to be published under their Veloce Publishing PLC imprint.

Many books have been written about the motorcycles of the fifties, yet, of the scene itself at that time, there have been very few. To attempt to do so from first-hand practical experience is not easy, because the passing years have tended to dull memories. Worse still, it is usually only the good things that are remembered and the bad forgotten. There is also always the danger of personal recollections becoming embroidered, distorted or just forgotten.

An awareness of these possible shortcomings prompted a considerable amount of research in old magazines and newspapers of that era, and many other sources, to ensure that what appears in print is as factually correct as possible. This, in itself, posed its own problems: so many long forgotten news items and features of almost fifty years ago were revealed whilst searching that the temptation to become sidetracked by them was hard to resist. Yet for all that it was, for me, largely a trip down memory lane, recalling many happenings that, in one way or the other, have left an indelible impression in my mind. That I shared those memories with a whole generation of motorcyclists has made this book possible.

I hope this book will also appeal to those who have joined motorcycling's ranks more recently. Riding an early postwar motorcycle today may help give an impression of what we once experienced, but it will fail to provide any real indication of the contemporary scene. They will not know what it was like having to run on the dreaded low octane 'pool' petrol, with its limitations on performance. Nor will they have called at a garage to get the engine oil topped up, to have it pumped up within a metal cabinet in the forecourt into a measuring can that sometimes contained dust, dead flies or other debris! Knowing no better, we took it all in our stride and revelled in the much lighter density of traffic on our roads, when motorways were unknown. We all believed implicitly everything we read in the two motorcycle weeklies of that era, which we regarded with reverence as the motorcyclist's bibles. They were, after all, written by people just like us.

To have covered the whole fifties scene in depth would have been a tremendous task, resulting in more than one volume. As a consequence, this book concentrates on certain topics which, when knitted together, provide a composite picture of the ten years during which the British motorcycle industry began to experience the wind of change. They were enjoyable days, as are all days with motorcycles and motorcyclists. I hope my recollections will be found just as pleasurable.

Jeff Clew
Sparkford, Somerset

Contents

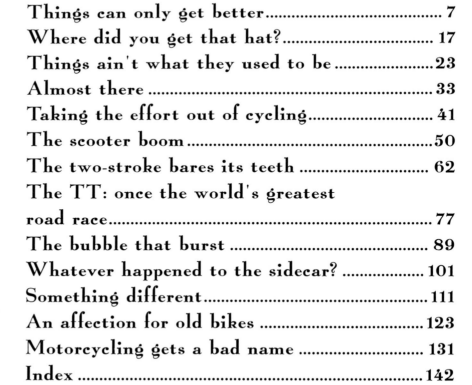

Things can only get better ...

At the beginning of 1950, the prospects for the forthcoming decade looked good, from the viewpoint of both the British motorcycle industry and the individual motorcyclist. Although Britain still needed to export as much as it could to aid the postwar recovery programme, new models - which previously had been destined for export only - were now becoming available to the home market, albeit in limited numbers. Interest centred mostly around the vertical twin which, in its most acceptable form, had been pioneered by Edward Turner when he launched his famous Triumph Speed Twin in 1937.

Most motorcyclists were optimistic in their outlook, believing that things could only get better, for already there were encouraging signs. This belief was upheld, for motorcycle production rose steadily from a total of 171,300 machines in 1950 to a peak of 234,000 in 1959. Even so, during the early fifties, those fortunate to be able to afford a new motorcycle often had to pay 'over the odds' to take priority on the waiting list of some of the more unscrupulous dealers. It was a repeat of what had happened after the 1914-18 war, when new models had been just as scarce. Those unable (or unwilling) to pay such a premium had either to sit it out and wait or make do with what they had. The only compromise was to purchase one of the many ex-War Department models that were now readily available at keen prices, some converted to civilian colours. Statistics show that in excess of 650,000 motorcycles were in use throughout the UK by the end of 1949, many of them of prewar or ex-WD origin.

It was not yet all plain sailing, however. By the beginning of 1951 an acute shortage of raw materials, especially sheet steel, was threatening to cut vehicle production by up to 50%. Already, domestic articles that used zinc, copper or tin in their manufacture had become virtually unobtainable. Ways had to be found to get around this problem by using alternative materials, although plastics could not be used for structural or load-bearing applications as they were not then suitable. For a time, cars and motorcycles began to appear with fewer

EVERY MAN'S CHOICE IN *New 1954 Motor Cycles*

Buy with Ease

Motorcycling in the 50s

PICK A WINNER FROM THE **FEARNLEY** STABLE— —ALL CHAMPIONS

The North's largest Distributors of all leading makes offer 100% satisfaction with more than

1,000 MACHINES
to select from

THESE INCLUDE :

ARIEL, ex-W.D., 350 c.c. O.H.V. de Luxe. Rebuilt by contractors for the Ministry of Supply regardless of cost. Meant for re-issue to H.M. Forces but never re-issued. These machines represent the finest value it has ever been our privilege to offer. £85 10 0
Deposit £21 10 0

INDIAN, 500 c.c. S.V. Twin. This substantially built transatlantic favourite is offered at practically half current list price. Reconditioned and equal to new. Re-cellulosed with an absolutely immaculate red finish. 40 only £85 0 0
Deposit £25 0 0

HARLEY DAVIDSON, 750 c.c. S.V. Twin. The Rolls Bentley of motor cycling. Unsurpassed for comfort and road holding. Finished in immaculate Green and Chrome they are the last word in luxury. Entirely rebuilt and offered as being equal to new £155 0 0
Deposit £55 0 0

First class spares and service departments, self-financed Hire Purchase, no fuss or harshness, but straightforward User-Rider Dealer understanding. Every Harley and Indian part in stock.

WRITE NOW FOR AN ADVANCE COPY OF OUR SPRING CATALOGUE

Fred
FEARNLEY LTD

692/4 ASHTON OLD ROAD, OPENSHAW, MANCHESTER 1
240 DEANSGATE, MANCHESTER

Fred Fearnley Ltd. of Manchester was typical of the dealers able to offer reconditioned ex-War Department machines in civilian colours, on hire purchase terms, if required.

plated parts which, in the case of the latter, took the form of painted, rather than plated, petrol tanks and wheel rims. This is a feature often overlooked by those who restore 1951/2 models to original specification.

As far as Clement Attlee's Labour government was concerned, a difficult and far-reaching decision had to be made as the car and motorcycle industries were major export earners. Already, bicycle manufacture had been cut by half and they were pondering over what cuts to make amongst the vehicle manufacturers when Washington came to their rescue by agreeing to supply Britain with 1,000,000 tons of steel.

Despite this welcome solution to the problem, new models were still difficult to come by, with most still destined for export as a priority. Second-hand models continued to fetch high prices as there was still heavy demand for them. Fortunately, this prospect was not quite as bad as it appeared at first sight. The tightening up of hire purchase regulations in North America seemed

As this Matchless advertisement shows, some machines previously available for export only were becoming available on the home market, too, by the early 1950s. (Courtesy Matchless Motorcycles Ltd.)

MOTOR CYCLE AGENTS

Models **G3/LS** *and* **G80S**

Available for export only during the 1949 season, the Models G3/LS 347 c.c. and G80S 498 c.c. are now being distributed to Home Dealers, and already riders in all parts of Great Britain are enjoying the unprecedented standard of steering and road-holding provided by the Matchless Patented system of full Teledraulic suspension

MAKE IT A MATCHLESS *SPRINGER* AND RIDE FARTHER FASTER

MATCHLESS
Clubman

MATCHLESS MOTOR CYCLES • PLUMSTEAD ROAD • LONDON. S.E.18.

likely to slow down the importation of new models into the USA; whilst this would damage the export trade, it would make more machines available on the home market.

The world-wide popularity of the British motorcycle meant that only a small number of foreign models had been imported into the UK during the prewar era. After the war, there was no question of further imports, no matter how small in number, being resumed. The European manufacturers were struggling to meet the demand of their own home market, many having had to re-start production from scratch. Imports from the USA were entirely out of the question as they would harm the balance of payments. It was not, therefore, until 1955 that imported machines began to arrive in significant numbers - almost 60,000 that year - after starting as a tiny trickle in 1952. Most of these were scooters and mopeds, by then very much in vogue.

With a less hidebound approach, many of the new imports - mostly from Germany and Italy - appealed a great deal to British enthusiasts, who were looking for something 'different'. The foreign imports provided a bright, colourful alternative, as well as a new approach to design, which compared well to the seemingly endless background of drab austerity during Britain's early postwar years. The tendency to 'buy foreign' gathered momentum and by 1959 imports had risen to a peak of 173,000. This was anything but welcome news to British manufacturers and the government, coinciding, as it did, with a marked fall in exports of British motorcycles. From a peak of almost 92,000 units in 1951 exports fell to 43,000 by 1959 and remained around this level for a further decade before shrinking even more.

A disturbing event that raised its head in 1951, and threatened exports to the USA, took the form of a petition to the US Tariff Commission by Harley-Davidson, whose aim it was to give substantial protection to the American motorcycle manufacturers. British motorcycles were being imported into America in ever-increasing numbers, having a harmful effect on domestic sales. As a consequence, Harley-Davidson requested the imposition of not only a 40% duty on all foreign motorcycle imports, but also a limit on the number of machines admitted, based on prewar shipments. If the case was upheld, it would ensure British-made motorcycles would no longer be a serious threat to their business and even close the American market to Britain altogether.

The case was successfully challenged on behalf of the British Motorcycle Dealers Association by its President, Dennis McCormack, the Triumph importer. Amongst the many points he raised was the fact that the American manufacturers had done virtually nothing to meet the British challenge, and did not have any of their own models with capacities to match most of the imported models. This, and some startling disclosures about the Milwaukee company's monopolistic marketing policies, led to the rejection of Harley-Davidson's petition. Under the Marshall Plan, foreign imports continued at a favourable tariff rate of 8% - and the British motorcycle industry (and the UK government!) heaved a sigh of relief.

The more stringently-applied hire purchase regulations in North America may have been seen by the British government as another means of reducing public spending, because it followed suit with new measures that came into effect on 29th January 1952. A new machine bought on hire purchase would now require a minimum deposit of 25%, with payment of the Purchase Tax in full. The amount outstanding would then have to be paid within twelve, eighteen or twenty four months. For a second-hand machine the minimum deposit

These two advertising posters give an indication of the impact made by successful British motorcycles in American competition events, even the spring frame 349cc ohv MAC Velocette. The Catalina Island race, off the coast of southern California, was regarded by many American enthusiasts as their country's equivalent of our own Isle of Man TT.

Motorcycling in the 50s

would be 25%, with the balance outstanding to be paid within twelve months. It hit the low wage earner particularly hard.

At the same time it was disclosed there would be a one third reduction in the number of machines available for sale in Britain, as compared to the production figures for 1951. Not unexpectedly, this placed an even higher premium on the value of second-hand models. The only good news, admittedly of little value to potential purchasers, was that export sales of motorcycles and bicycles had reached a record level of £42,000,000 during the previous year.

At the beginning of 1950, petrol was still rationed, with a meagre allowance that varied according to a machine's capacity, but which would permit about 90 miles of travel a month. A supplementary allowance could be applied for in cases of hardship and, inevitably, there was always the 'black market'. Petrol coupons could always be bought if the prospective purchaser was prepared to pay the price. However, if it were found that petrol intended for commercial use was being used for unauthorised private travel, the offender could end up in court. Spot checks were easy to make, as petrol for commercial use was dyed red. Many ingenious methods were devised for removing the dye, one allegedly by filtering it through a loaf of bread!

The only petrol available was what was known as 'pool' petrol, a low-grade fuel with an octane rating in the low seventies. The engines of the more sporting type of machine loathed it and needed to be set up carefully if they were to run reasonably well. Pre-ignition problems were rife and the exhaust valve led a hard life. Whatever the type of engine, some loss in performance was inevitable.

Ironically, petrol had by now become freely available in most of the Continental countries, with even Germany due to abandon petrol rationing during February. This became a bone of contention amongst the British motoring community and gave rise to questions in the House of Commons. The Labour Government claimed that if more petrol was imported from the USA, it would not only erode the balance of payments but also harm the export drive. The pressure continued to mount and, when Germany ended rationing, the Government was forced to relent. As a result, petrol rationing in Britain came to an end on the eve of the 1950 Whitsun Bank Holiday. There was a sting in the tail, however: provision had been made in the April budget to increase the tax on petrol by 9d (4p) a gallon. Regarded by many as another form of rationing - by price - Sir Stafford Cripps, Labour's Chancellor of the Exchequer, had the gall to say he saw nothing unusual in any proposal to raise tax, if it was considered necessary. It was he who, in 1947, had made his infamous 'tighten your belts' speech.

Sadly, petrol rationing made an unwelcome return several years later. When the Suez crisis flared up in 1956, the supply of fuel from the Middle East was disrupted and rationing

When petrol rationing was re-introduced as a result of the 1956 Suez crisis, a machine of over 250cc capacity was entitled to double the allowance of one under 250cc. The coupon book shown was never used, however, as rationing ended during mid-May 1957.

Things can only get better ...

had to be re-introduced on 17th December that year. The production of 100 octane fuel was suspended altogether but, as far as the petrol allowance was concerned, a more generous mileage of about 800 miles a month was possible. Even so, a couple of months elapsed before the government conceded there was a case for an allowance of petrol so that selected competition events could continue. By 17th April 1957, the Middle East situation had eased sufficiently for the petrol allowance to be increased by 50% and, by 15th May, rationing came to an end.

Branded petrol became available on 1st February 1953. By then, a whole new generation of motorists and motorcyclists had the freedom of choice for the first time and the advertising agencies enjoyed a bonanza. No-one mourned the passing of the infamous 'pool'. Engine development was no longer handicapped, as the higher octane fuels would permit higher compression ratios to be used. As a consequence, the now more efficient engines had not only enhanced performance but better fuel economy, too.

Prospects for touring abroad opened up, even though, initially, currency regulations restricted the amount of money that could be taken out of the country. Ken and Mollie Craven had been quick to see encouraging prospects for foreign travel on two wheels if it were properly co-ordinated and soon became well-known for their Partitours. As an offspring of this, the Craven name became even better known, through the purpose-built and stylish luggage-carrying equipment, which went a long way toward making the motorcycle tourist respectable. The days of insecurely-mounted and rattling ex-WD pannier frames, with their scruffy and anything but waterproof army packs, were numbered!

Oil was still dispensed from garage forecourts in a somewhat primitive manner. When calling for a top-up, it was cranked up from a metal cabinet into a measuring can, from which the attendant would pour it direct into the oil tank. Otherwise, pint, quart or gallon tins were the order of the day. In cold weather, the task of cranking up the oil was not made easier by the now viscous oil, for at that time multi-grade oils were unknown. The day of the 'do-it-yourself' can, with its tear-off sealing strip, was still some way off, although Esso marketed its oils in embossed, clear glass bottles, that have today become collectors' items. For those who

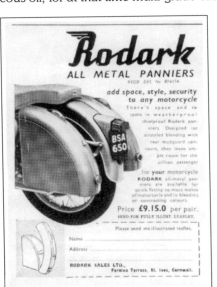

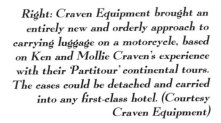

Right: Craven Equipment brought an entirely new and orderly approach to carrying luggage on a motorcycle, based on Ken and Mollie Craven's experience with their 'Partitour' continental tours. The cases could be detached and carried into any first-class hotel. (Courtesy Craven Equipment)

Left: Rodark Sales Ltd. entered the luggage-carrying market later with its own stylish pannier equipment which followed the contours of the machine's rear mudguard.

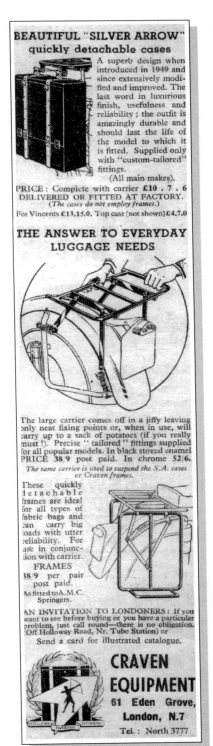

Motorcycling in the 50s

This Castrol advertisement of the fifties is based on the familiar measuring can used to top up the oil of a motorcycle or a car. (Courtesy Castrol (UK) Ltd.)

A later version of Castrol's 'oil bar' with gauges to show the amount of oil pumped into the oil can. Note the inevitable Redex upper cylinder 'oil squirt' in the background and also the protective pad to prevent petrol spillage onto paintwork from the petrol pump's hose. (Courtesy Castrol (UK) Ltd.)

ran two-strokes, for which oil and petrol had to be pre-mixed, it was usually a case of adding the correct measure of oil after the petrol tank had been filled, then shaking the machine vigorously to mix it!

During the spring and autumn, car and motorcycle owners had to perform the regular ritual of changing the engine oil to a thicker or thinner sort to keep pace with seasonal temperature changes. Until multi-grade oils arrived on to the market, oils were usually of the monograde type, although in the early fifties it was common practice to include detergents in their formulation to help keep the engine internals cleaner.

Few books about motorcycling were available at this time, apart from those published by either Iliffe or Temple Press. If technical advice had to be sought over and above that provided by the manufacturer's own instruction book (the quality of which was by no means consistent), *Pitman's Motor-Cyclists Library* or *Pearson's Motor Cycle Repair* series of books offered the only real alternatives. The day of the proprietary, well-illustrated step-by-step D-I-Y workshop manual, had yet to dawn. Required reading amongst motorcyclists invariably took the form of the two weekly magazines, *The Motor Cycle* and *Motor Cycling*, known respectively as the 'blue 'un' and the 'green 'un' on account of the colour of their front covers. Both were published on a Thursday and woe betide the newspaper boy who failed to deliver one of them on publication day or, worse still, both! Many enthusiasts bought both, or else exchanged one for the other with a friend. They were read avidly from cover to cover as soon as they had popped through the letterbox.

The road tests published in these magazines would carry little credence today, as any untoward criticism was toned down to prevent the loss of advertising revenue. A case in point is that of Associated Motor Cycles, who took

Esso supplied lubricating oil in glass bottles, stored in racks on the garage forecourt, as shown here. When branded petrol was re-introduced on 1st February 1953, filling stations stayed open for long hours and were a blaze of light. (Courtesy Esso UK plc).

exception to a report published by *Motor Cycling* during 1941 which was critical of its new military model. For many years afterwards, the company refused to supply AJS or Matchless motorcycles for road test by the press. It was a somewhat short-sighted reaction that must have cost it sales in the long run.

With a little experience, the regular reader soon learnt to read between the lines of what actually appeared in print and to realise that some of the text was couched in terms of which an estate agent's copywriter would have been proud. For example, 'slight vibration was experienced at normal cruising speed' would often mean it had been severe enough to loosen fillings in the rider's teeth! There appeared many oft-repeated cliches, too, such as 'the clutch was progressive in action and took up the drive smoothly'. Yet, for all that, the standard of journalism was high with a complete absence of expletives, slang and Americanisms.

Of the two magazines, *The Motor Cycle* (an Iliffe publication) was re-

Motorcycling in the 50s

garded as the more authoritative, being more formal in text composition and layout. This does not imply, however, that *Motor Cycling* (published by Temple Press) was in any way inferior. Quite to contrary; it was preferred by the clubman type of rider, who found its light-hearted and less patronising approach more acceptable. It is probably fair to say each magazine reflected the personality of its editor at that time: Arthur Bourne of *The Motor Cycle* and Graham Walker of *Motor Cycling*, who were followed by Harry Louis and Bob Holliday respectively.

The first issue of a new motorcycling tabloid, *Motor Cycle News*, was published on 30th November 1955, and was edited by Cyril Quantrill, a former *Motor Cycling* staffman, aided by Roger Maughfling, formerly of *The Motor Cycle*. Of eight pages initially, the publication soon found its own niche and has continued in print, long after the two older and much revered magazines ceased publication.

The advent of *Motor Cycle News* (which was published on a Wednesday), later acquired by the East Midland Allied Press, meant the two motorcycling weeklies lost their long-held duopoly. This was further eroded during the late fifties when two new motorcycling monthlies appeared on the scene: *Motor Cycle Mechanics* and *Motor Cyclist Illustrated*. Long before this, a motoring magazine, *Practical Motorist*, purported to show an interest in motorcycles by incorporating the words 'and Motor Cyclist' in its title. Edited by the redoubtable F.J. Camm, whose name appeared as editor of many other practical works, the first issue was published in May 1954. It is doubtful, however, whether many copies were bought by motorcyclists. Apart from the somewhat bland road tests that appeared in early issues, there was little else of specific interest to them as it was merely a regurgitation of what others had written in the past.

As mentioned earlier, Iliffe and Temple Press each had a good range of books about motorcycling, some of them having been published when the motorcycle was little more than a novelty. These titles had been updated regularly and, to quote one example, *Motorcycles and How to Manage Them* had reached its 32nd edition by 1953, underlining its popularity. A significant addition to the Iliffe list was made in 1950, when Canon B.H. Davies, the doyen of all motorcycling authors who wrote under the pseudonym *Ixion*, had his book *Motor Cycle Cavalcade* published. It summarised, through his personal involvement, the history of motorcycling in a vivid manner and contained a potted history of the better-known marques.

The many newcomers to motorcycling were unable to make any comparison with the way things were immediately before the war, but for those who were already riding then it was evident a great deal of change had taken place. Having suffered for so many years from lack of development, the lightweight two-stroke had, by the mid-fifties, begun to cast off its image of a cheap means of commuting to and from work, or a convenient entry point to motorcycling. At last its capabilities were being recognised and it was beginning to assert itself in competition events, as shown in a later chapter.

At the beginning of the fifties, the sports type of motorcycle could still be ridden to and from work during the week, then entered in a trial or a scramble at weekends. It was a situation that was soon to change when machines designed specially for competition use came into fashion. It was not so easy to ride in grass track or scrambles events during the summer, or in trials during the winter, without having two machines. A scrambles model, for example, was then only suitable for this type of event and would be hopeless if ridden in

a trial. When this happened, riders no longer rode these bikes on the road, or to and from a meeting, using instead a van or a sidecar outfit fitted with two planks on which the bike was tied. Society was becoming more affluent and, as this happened, motorcycle sport became less of an all-round activity, developing instead into each of its separate spheres.

Other trends, hitherto unknown, began to emerge, too. The scooter boom, as reported elsewhere, encouraged a whole new generation of riders - who otherwise would never have considered buying a conventional motorcycle - to take to two wheels. The latter, in their eyes, were looked upon as dirty, noisy and in need of constant attention, whereas the scooter was perceived as something chic with good weather protection - a fun machine that would make them less dependent on public transport. Needless to say, scooters were despised by the dyed-in-the-wool average motorcyclist, an unfortunate by-product of which led to the emergence of the 'mod' and 'rocker' cults which did little to enhance the good image of two-wheel enthusiasts in general. When the bubble car appeared, it presented an alternative to the sidecar outfit and affected sales of the latter.

The cafe racer was another trend of the fifties, a class of machine difficult to describe as it appeared in so many different guises. It was not a new trend, as there was evidence of its existence well before World War 2. It came about because motorcyclists wished to make their machines more distinctive, far removed from the appearance of the standard production models. Using the now almost extinct roadside cafes as their rendezvous, the cafe racers rode some remarkably well-engineered 'specials', thanks to the provision of all manner of 'bolt-on' goodies usually made by motorcyclists who were also engineers. They gave a machine a more sporting image and often even improved performance.

The cafe racer trend coincided so well with the rock-and-roll era that it formed the spearhead of the rocker cult, engendering a feeling of antipathy toward scooter riders. Unfortunately, the advent of the cafe racers did little to enhance the image of motorcycling. Often anti-social behaviour and more than a sprinkling of fatalities meant the fraternity was regarded as outlaws, viewed in much the same light as the characters depicted in the Marlon Brando

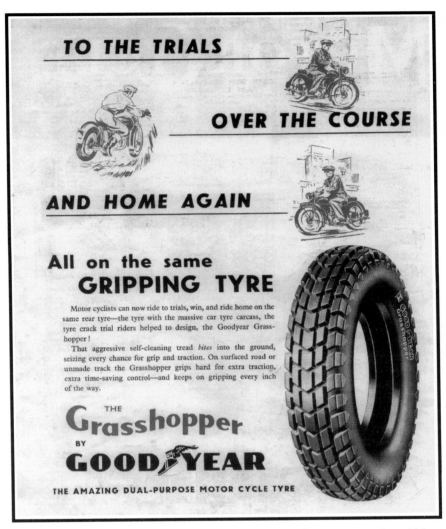

In an era when a motorcycle could be ridden on or off road with only minor modification, the Goodyear Grasshopper tyre meant a change was no longer necessary before riding in a trial. (Courtesy Goodyear Great Britain Ltd)

Motorcycling in the 50s

film of 1954, *The Wild One* . Yet, for all that, the trend caught on to such an extent, even if it was shunned by the two weekly magazines, that some of the manufacturers could no longer ignore it. Towards the end of that decade and well into the sixties, factory-made cafe racers could be purchased over the counter, initially from British manufacturers, but later from the Italians, before the former were emasculated and killed off by their Japanese contemporaries.

Today, the trend is still regarded with affection by some of its former - but now much older - fellowship and has led to a number of nostalgic "Rockers Reunions" in recent years.

With the blacker side of motorcycling attracting the attention of the media against a backdrop of rising concern about the ever-mounting toll of fatalities and serious injuries, these self-inflicted wounds served only to strengthen a new anti-motorcycling lobby. As a later chapter will show, motorcycling's image was becoming badly tarnished which, in the fullness of time, would prove increasingly disadvantageous. As a result, many came to regard motorcyclists as little more than social outcasts and the whole movement suffered badly.

Apart from the foregoing, things had generally improved by the mid-fifties, a trend that continued until 1959, when a peak figure of 331,806 new motorcycles were registered that year. The total number of motorcycles then in use had also risen to 1.75 million.

Where did you get that hat?

One of the greatest problems facing the early postwar rider was finding outer clothing to wear on the bike that was waterproof, warm and not too expensive. As little had been made specifically for this purpose after the war, it was a question of visiting one of the many army surplus stores that had sprung up all over the country and buying what appeared to offer the best solution.

To the uninitiated, an ex-War Department flying suit, tank suit or similar garment, seemed to provide the answer for a modest outlay. In most cases these suits would certainly keep the rider warm although, unfortunately, they were not waterproof. A tank suit, for example, was lined with kapok, an excellent insulant which, when wet, absorbed water like a sponge. In no time at all, the weight of the waterlogged suit was more like that worn by a deep sea diver!

If sartorial elegance was of little consequence and the need to keep dry all-important, the answer lay in what was known as a submarine suit. A two-piece suit, it was made from the now familiar waxed cotton cloth, unlined, and black in colour. Each half was made in one piece, with no zips or buttons, the top half - which had to be pulled on over the head - was cut so squarely that it looked like a coal sack with arms. Inelegant it may have been, and difficult to see in the dark, but at least it kept out the water, for a time.

The more impecunious bought a thin but all-enveloping gas cape, which was worn over the usual outer clothing. It, too, kept out the rain, but once the rider was on the move it billowed out like a balloon, creating a passable impression of Bibendum, the Michelin man.

Despatch rider's coats were better, but heavy and not particularly flexible. The seasoned rider tended to rely on old and well-proven rubber waders if they were still serviceable, worn in conjunction with a multi-layer full-length coat. The latter were known as 'footing coats', as they made it difficult for an observer to see whether a trials rider had dabbed or footed whilst negotiating a section. They were well made and had a button-up 'tummy pad' to provide

An ex-War Department tank suit, ex-RAF Mark VII goggles and ex-RAF gloves - all he could afford at the time (after all, his 1914 Triumph had cost him all of £5!) - formed the author's riding ensemble in this early postwar Pioneer Run. The tank suit (and the gloves) were definitely NOT waterproof.

Motorcycling in the 50s

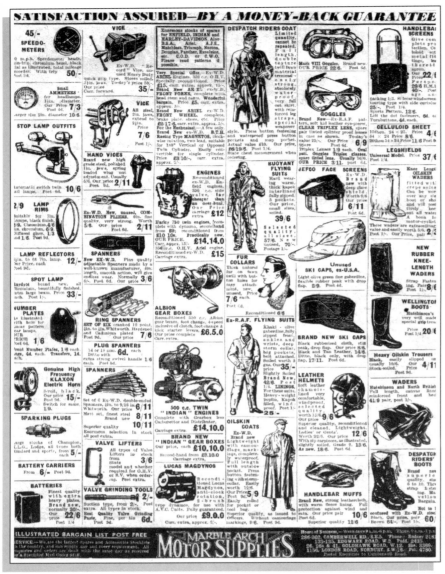

Whatever you needed, be it ex-WD clothing or just a spare part, Marble Arch Motor Supplies was likely to have it at a bargain price.

Right: Marcus Stores of Gravesend, Kent was one of many outlets that sold a very extensive range of ex-WD clothing.

extra warmth where it was most needed. They were heavy, too, due to their multi-layer construction, and not at all easy to carry about. They could also become unbearably hot during moments of extreme exertion, such as when trying to kickstart a machine reluctant to fire. Ex-US

Where did you get that hat?

19'6 SECURES THE FAMOUS 'CLUBMAN' Suit

BALANCE OVER 6 MONTHS

NOW IMMEDIATELY AVAILABLE FROM STOCK.

Made from 100 per cent. Waterproof black tough NON-CRACKING THORNHIDE material of the type recently tested for the ADMIRALTY.

★ Stitched and high frequency treated seams throughout.
★ Jacket fleece lined with two large hip pockets and full length frontal zip covered by 6in. storm flap.
★ Large storm collar and throat tab.
★ Gusseted cuffs.
★ Press studs throughout.
★ Trousers fleece lined and cut to give easy movement, fitted with belted waist and ankle straps.
★ Suitable for ladies' wear.

By the mid-50s, two-piece suits were becoming popular. Pride and Clarke Ltd. (always referred to irreverently as Pride and Shark!) could offer a Clubman suit for £6.6s cash, or on the 'easy terms' for which the company was renowned, on payment of a deposit of 19/6d, with the balance payable over six months.

forces garments probably offered the best compromise, especially the leather flying jackets with their fur collar and lining. Unfortunately, they tended to be expensive, were not waterproof and not easy to find in good condition.

When plastic coats and suits eventually arrived on the market they were mostly made from pvc-coated fabric. Through the use of an unsuitable plasticiser and the inability of the fabric to breathe, they became rock hard in winter and unbearably hot in summer. Most of the other, perhaps more suitable, plastic-coated fabrics were, like new motorcycles, ear-marked for export.

Messrs. Pride and Clarke, the one-time well-known south London dealer, came up with an ultra-light-weight 'Packaway' oversuit, which offered good protection from the wet at a low price. Compact, it could be carried in the small haversack pro-

Armadrake was one of several motorcycle clothing manufacturers who, in the mid-50s, could offer a truly waterproof coat with a detachable lining for under £11.

Armadrake RANGE!

The garments on this page are specially designed to give the Armadrake standard of protection to riders whose financial resources fall short of the complete luxury of the 'Meteor'.

The Viscount £5·18·11

FINE TEXTURE GABERDINE—in itself resistant to moisture and, in addition, chemically-and-rubber-proofed. Specially designed "through-back" allows free circulation of air. Underarm vents provide further ventilation. Windproof throatpiece. Heavy blended-woollen lining throughout the coat. One-piece sleeve. Tummy Pad and Leg Tabs. Leatherbound cuffs and pockets. Deep Storm Collar, Capacious side-pockets and Breast map-pocket.

The Viking £7·15·0

The Viking Suit is excellently tailored in heavy quality proofed gaberdine, with heavy blended-woollen lining. Also has full-length zip-fastener and press studs; elastic-waisted trousers; reinforced seat and knees; snug-fitting adjustable strap collar; strap-and-buckle ankle grip; leather-bound cuffs. Price complete £7.15.0 or—

SEPARATELY:
Jacket £4.13.6. Chest 34" to 44"
Trousers £3.6.0. I. Leg 28", 30", 32"

★ Literature Post Free! Descriptive folders and leaflets sent on request. Also obtainable from your local dealers.

Sole Manufacturers: S. H. Whyman Ltd., St. Peter's Place, Leeds 9.

the famous BELSTAFF range

WORN BY MOTOR-CYCLISTS ALL THE WORLD OVER

'Look for THE BELSTAFF BRAND Your Sure Guarantee

Belstaff, yet another well-known motorcycle clothing manufacturer, catered for all tastes. The range included ladies waterproof clothing in various styles and sizes, all at the same price. (Courtesy Phoenix Distribution (NW) Ltd.)

vided, but being made from thin, rubberised fabric meant it tore easily and would perish if not dried out correctly. Its bright canary yellow colour suggested it had started life as a dinghy suit, intended to be stowed away in aircraft and be conspicuous if the crew had to ditch in the sea. Later, Pride and Clarke offered its own, two-piece "Clubman" suit, which paved the way for other proprietary suits. By then, the old and well-established multi-layer, full-length coats were back in production, with the choice of a Belstaff, Stormgard or Armadrake for around £10, or from newcomers such as Feridax and Bell.

Gradually, the stock of ex-WD clothing began to dry up, although the ex-Navy flight deck suit available from Claude Rye, another one-time well-known south London dealer, lingered on. Also popular was the Army's three-quarter length combat jacket, which many ladies found attractive.

For the ladies, the choice of what to wear in the early fifties was even less flattering, if that was possible. Most pinned their faith in a good outer coat, even an ex-Land Army coat, which they wore in conjunction with jodhpurs and lace-up riding boots. A headscarf or a close-fitting white coloured leather helmet of the type worn by aviators completed the ensemble.

Headgear styles amongst the menfolk varied, too. For a while, ex-RAF leather flying helmets were very popular, though not very becoming. They helped keep the ears warm in cold weather but, being made of soft leather, were not waterproof. Others resorted to the time-honoured flat cap held in place by goggles (often worn with the peak at the back!), a beret of some kind, or a ski cap with extendable ear flaps, so beloved of the sidecar driver that it virtually became his trademark.

Very little interest was shown in safety helmets initially, and some time would pass before, in 1962, it became mandatory to wear one. There were only a few manufacturers to begin with, although the situation began to change when increasing concern was shown about the high incidence of head injuries in motorcycle accidents. The two weekly magazines began to encourage the use of helmets by adopting a 'you know it makes sense' attitude, ensuring their staff always wore them in photographs. It was hoped that if sufficient

Where did you get that hat?

numbers of riders were seen wearing helmets it would avert the threat of compulsion. A type known as the Corker - similar to that worn by the police - proved especially popular and the old bike enthusiast had the option of buying one that was a good representation of a deerstalker hat.

An unwritten code of etiquette meant that riders who rode their machines to and from a competition event stripped off all the legal requirements and replaced them before riding home. It was not the done thing to be seen wearing a helmet on the public highway; it had to be strapped to the machine, or carried in a haversack (and any racing number plates obscured by covering them with paper!)

Footwear usually took the form of despatch riders' boots, with their laces and straps, or pull-on firemens' boots. These were the norm in grass track and scrambles events, worn in conjunction with an ex-WD battledress top, jodhpurs and an AC-U approved helmet, where they formed the minimum obligatory requirement. Being cheap and in plentiful supply, the boots, jacket and jodhpurs were in common use on the road, too. Wellington boots were never well-suited to motorcycling, affording little protection in the event of a spill and too clumsy for any proper feel of the rear brake and gearchange pedals. They were bitterly cold in winter, too, whilst the open top formed a rain funnel unless leggings could be stretched over them. Being thin, the leggings would then split!

When Dunlop introduced calf-length, zip-up overboots, it answered the footwear problem for many. Until then, those who wore normal footwear found it necessary to carry overshoes, should it rain. Many relied on another item of anti-gas equipment; voluminous calf-length overshoes made of oilskin that resembled elephant's feet until tightened up by canvas straps. Eventually, zip-up fashion-style boots, either lined or unlined, became readily available, but only in black.

Gloves and goggles also presented problems at first. Ex-RAF gauntlet-type chrome leather flying gloves were very popular, and in winter could provide reasonable warmth worn with white silk inners, also ex-RAF. Although not waterproof, they did incorporate built-in heating elements, unfortunately not designed for use with a 6 volt electrical system. Cold hands were *de rigueur* and frequently motorcyclists were seen stopped by the wayside indulging in the 'cab driver's fling' in an effort to restore circulation!

The RAF provided the best goggles, too, the rigid Mark VII type with separate two-angled laminated glass lenses and a padded leather surround, or the flexible but more expensive Mark VIII version, the centre between the lenses of which was adjustable. Anti-gas goggles with a flimsy celluloid lens dominated the market, being cheap, expendable and light to wear. Later, when the single plastic lens type of goggle came into fashion, a deeper-bodied version fulfilled a long-awaited need of spectacle wearers. Rain or misting up was always a problem, though, one type having a projecting plastic extension with a narrow aperture at its end. Another had a metallic eye coverage into which elongated slits had been cut. Their use must surely have been legally questionable ...

The alternative to goggles was a visor, a hinged, semi-circular band of stiff, transparent plastic, attached to a safety helmet. These were very different from the type of visor used today in conjunction with a full-face helmet, but suffered from similar disadvantages. They would scratch easily and, when marked in any way, would 'star' in either bright sunlight or the dark when faced with the

This IS my cup of tea!

The CORKER PROTECTIVE HELMET

Obtainable from all main dealers, at 65/- complete

Of the few safety helmets worn initially, the Corker seemed to be the most popular; those coloured black worn by the menfolk and white-coloured ones by the ladies. The London Metropolitan Police wore black Corker helmets, too.

The Olicana Windshield was a great favourite of LE Velocette riders for it afforded good weather protection above the LE's built-in legshields, although would reduce the top speed noticeably.

Is YOUR machine fitted with a

OLICANA WINDSHIELD

If not there are

Models to fit all types of motor cycles, prices from £4/10/6 to £6/10/-. De Luxe models have the centre panel cellulosed in any colour preferred, with an aluminium beading. Service and satisfaction guaranteed. See your dealer today or write for details to:

OLICANA PRODUCTS
ILKLEY, YORKS   Tel.: ILKLEY 1375

21

Motorcycling in the 50s

Whilst working for the Distillers Plastics Group during his early career, the author was persuaded to model this Comet two-piece suit made by P. and L. Suswin, of Clacton-on-Sea, Essex, which he was allowed to keep as a 'perk'. His 1938 KSS seen behind is fitted with a Craven rear carrier.

headlamps of oncoming vehicles.

It is, perhaps, appropriate to mention here weather protection on the machine itself. Until the introduction of fibreglass made fairings a reality, such protection as existed took the form of metal legshields, heavily valanced mudguards and a Perspex screen attached to the handlebars by a system of rods and clamps. There were also lined muffs that could be attached to the end of the handlebars to keep the rider's hands warm. Warm, waterproof clothing was still the basic requirement. Owners of an LE Velocette probably enjoyed the most effective compromise as they could fit a large screen, marketed under the Olicana name. It had a fabric apron attached to bridge the gap between the screen and the machine's in-built legshields, and provided almost total frontal protection. Unfortunately, it also reduced top speed.

When fibreglass mouldings became a practical proposition, fairings came into fashion. Available in all shapes and sizes (some offering only minimal protection and others providing almost complete protection for rider and machine) they were attached to the machine by a system of clamps and stays and were relatively easy to remove, when required, although the more enveloping types necessitated first detaching the front wheel.

Firm attachment was necessary to prevent them from flapping, and there never seemed to be a satisfactory way of transferring the front of the headlamp to the front of a fairing. Because the fairing and its screen had to be mounted some way ahead of the front fork, transferral of the reflector unit left the inner of the headlamp shell open and exposed, protected only by the moulding some way from it. It also called for unsightly long and straggling leads to the light unit, rather like a series of coloured umbilical cords.

As many found to their displeasure, a fairing tended to amplify engine noise, directing it upward to the rider's ears. Many a machine that was previously considered mechanically quiet sounded alarmingly noisy after a fairing had been attached. It could also, under some circumstances, trap a rider in an accident, who otherwise might have been thrown clear.

The search for warmth, refuge from a soaking, comfort and, above all else, style was only just beginning in the fifties. How different it must have seemed to the motorcyclist when he espied the scooterist in helmet and duffle coat or parka, seemingly impervious to the weather. Scooters were born with a protective front apron and a screen was easily fitted. The European accessory manufacturers soon saw the opening that the demand for good quality aftermarket fittings created. One look at a set of Craven panniers, or their equivalent metal quarter segment design made by Rodark, illustrates a revolution had occurred in luggage-carrying equipment. When German visitors to the 1959 TT showed off the first tank top bags, there was no holding back. It showed motorcyclists could be neat and tidy, too!

Things ain't what they used to be

At the time of the 1951 Motor Cycle Show (there was no show in 1950), 37 manufacturers and concessionaires of motorcycles were listed as exhibitors. Fears were expressed that this number was likely to decrease by the end of the decade; a fear by no means unjustified. However, whilst takeovers and failures to continue trading reduced the number as anticipated, it was offset by an apparent increase in numbers due, in the main, to the increasing number of foreign manufacture motorcycle, scooter and moped concessionaires. Toward the end of the decade, imports were accounting for more than four times the number of British machines exported; not good news for the government or the industry.

The widespread adoption of the telescopic front fork placed more emphasis on rider comfort to the extent that some form of rear suspension was now considered just as desirable. It would certainly be of benefit to the long-suffering pillion passenger who, more often than not, perched on a tiny pillion seat filled with sorbo rubber, the equivalent of an upholstered brick! Among the larger capacity models, spring frame options were becoming available in almost every manufacturer's range, intended to phase out the rigid frame completely. In due course the lightweight two-strokes followed suit, so that rigid frames became a relic of the past. Almost all had already changed to an undamped telescopic front fork.

Some manufacturers, such as Ariel, BSA and Norton, remained faithful to the older, plunger type rear suspension as long as they could. At its best, it provided only a compromise with its limited movement, lack of damping and, as wear began to set in, deterioration in handling. Only Ariel showed some initiative by incorporating what was known as an Anstey link to help keep constant the tension of the final drive chain. Triumph, meanwhile, blithely ploughed on with its unconventional spring wheel. An ingenious device designed by Edward Turner, it had the advantage of instantly converting a rigid

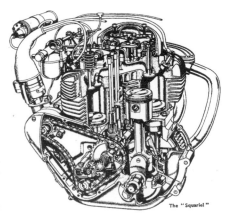

The "Squariel"

Motorcycling in the 50s

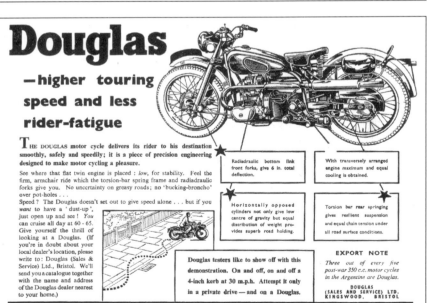

frame without need for drastic surgery, and would take the worst out of some of the larger bumps. The Mark I version was alleged to add only 12lbs in extra weight.

However, it, too, was not the complete answer. Other manufacturers, such as Associated Motor Cycles, Royal Enfield and Velocette, saw better prospects in pivoted fork rear suspension, its movement controlled by hydraulically-damped rear suspension units. It seemed the only sensible way to go, having been used successfully by Velocette on the 1936 works racers. Their judgement proved correct, as it eventually became the accepted norm. Each of these companies had used this type of rear suspension when they first began to make spring frames - and had a head start when most of their contemporaries changed from plunger suspension in 1953. There were, however, two notable exceptions.

Douglas and Vincent adopted their own individual approach to the problem. George Halliday had been assessing the potential of torsion bar suspension for the postwar horizontally-opposed Douglas twin. His arrangement gave the rear wheel a movement of up to six inches and provided the works testers with their 'party piece': the ability to ride up and down a kerb at 30mph! It was a feat no other manufacturer could match at that time. Even this form of rear suspension had its drawbacks. Apart from the need to grease, at regular intervals, the joints of the bell crank arrangement that linked the swinging arm fork with the longitudinal torsion bars, it was undamped. When carrying a pillion passenger it worked well, but when the machine was ridden solo it sometimes behaved more like a pogo stick on uneven surfaces.

Philip Vincent possessed a wealth of experience of spring frame designs, in which he had specialised since acquiring HRD in 1927, the company that eventually bore his own name. The Vincent cantilever design was controlled by twin suspension units, a more sophisticated version of which, with only a single central unit, is used by most of today's manufacturers. Vincent also had its own version of front fork on some models, the Girdraulic, which represented a cross between a girder and a telescopic front fork with hydraulic damping.

During this period of increasing production, the British motorcycle industry was able to pay little attention to new designs to such an extent that there was no incentive to hold a Motor Cycle Show in 1950. Because the industry could sell everything it made there was no inclination to spend time and money on entirely new designs. Although this philosophy would have a familiar ring about it in later years, it would be unfair at this time to accuse the industry of complacency so soon after the war. Most manufacturers had overflowing order books and a waiting list of customers on the home market. To cite one example, Triumph found it necessary to tone down its advertising, otherwise it was in danger of creating additional demand it could not hope to fulfil. With already a waiting list of enthusiastic customers, and aware of the need to keep the name in the forefront, Triumph adopted a subtle but humorous approach. A series of cartoon-type advertisements by Alex Oxley, renowned for his contributions to *Motor Cycling*, showed how easy it was on a Triumph.

The purchase price of all new machines increased by no less than one third

Philip Vincent had the foresight to persist with his cantilever suspension system which is in widespread use today, though in a modified form. He could justly claim his 998cc Black Shadow vee twin was the world's fastest standard production motorcycle. Did anyone else ever get so many words into a single page advertisement?

IT'S EASY ON A TRIUMPH

Anyone who read Motor Cycling *during the early postwar years will recall Alex Oxley's cartoons only too readily. He had the knack of being able to portray down to the smallest detail the more amusing side of motorcycling, with which we could ourselves identify. It was a brilliant move by Triumph to involve him in its 'soft sell' advertising campaign. (Courtesy Triumph Motorcycles Ltd.)*

due to the iniquitous Purchase Tax. Many people expected this punitive tax to be repealed soon after the war had ended but, like most taxes, it continued for a long while afterwards. When eventually it was removed, it was instantly replaced by VAT!

A curious practice of some manufacturers was to list a speedometer amongst the optional extras, even though its fitment was a legal requirement! It, too, carried Purchase Tax, as did a pillion seat and footrests, also listed as optional extras but mandatory if a pillion passenger was carried. Velocette set a good example by including the cost of a licence holder, pillion seat and footrests and a speedometer in the purchase price. They had done so before the war.

Not everyone, of course, could afford a new motorcycle, but the telescopic fork made such an impact that many were anxious to replace the now outmoded girder fork with one. It was a relatively easy task in most cases, necessitating changing the diameter of the head race bearings and possibly compensating for a change in the length of the steering head stem. The Matchless Teledraulic front fork was the one most frequently fitted and, as a result, whenever an ex-WD G3/L Matchless was broken for spares, the fork was the first part to be sold. It also meant fitting the matching front wheel and often the need to change the point from which the speedometer was driven. Not every such conversion was a success, unfortunately. Unwarranted changes in the steering geometry could have an adverse effect on handling, transforming a machine that once handled well into one that was decidedly imprecise. Furthermore, some of the early telescopic front forks were not too well damped and would dip noticeably under heavy braking.

There was also a roaring trade in rear suspension conversions, where all manner of proprietary rear ends were grafted on. Some, such as the McCandless and McKenzie, enjoyed a good reputation, whereas some of the others were not too well thought out and added unnecessary weight. A few converted to plunger-type rear suspension, which was an easier modification to make but offered little advantage. There was even a rival to Triumph's spring wheel - the Clamil.

Machines converted in these ways lost a great deal of their originality, which at the time caused little concern. With the vintage machine cult growing, however, many valuable and sometimes historic motorcycles suffered in this manner. No-one bothered to keep the old girder fork, which was usually consigned for scrap, for it seemed inconceivable that the need would ever arise to convert back to the maker's original specification. If it did, as often happened much later when full-scale restorations were undertaken, finding the correct original parts became an increasingly difficult problem.

A by-product of this was that almost everyone disposed of the saddle and separate pillion seat when the dualseat came into fashion. With a spring frame conversion, a dualseat provided the finishing touch, improving the look of the machine and in its comfort. It was only too easy to overlook the fact that when one was fitted to a rigid frame bike the only springing provided would be that of the front fork. The rider and his passenger now absorbed most of the road shocks - and suffered accordingly. One or two of the more perceptive dualseat makers, such as Milverton, were aware of this problem and offered a dualseat with mattress-type spring internals, which provided a satisfactory compromise. As in the case of the old girder forks, saddles and pillion seats were also discarded whenever dualseats replaced them. They, too, became difficult to find and in recent years have been re-manufactured to meet demand from vintage machine restorers.

Other improvements followed, such as the replacement of the old-established Type 276 Amal carburetter by that company's Monobloc design in 1955. It provided an altogether neater arrangement, having the float chamber as an integral part of the main body casting.

The electrics also received attention. The hitherto rather unreliable d.c. system, with its separate dynamo and magneto, was replaced by an alternator and coil ignition. Many regarded this as a retrograde step, especially those who had suffered problems with coil ignition in earlier times when it relied on an overworked d.c. dynamo and battery. The alternator represented a considerable step forward, with its greater charging rate, windings that no longer rotated and, eventually, the ability to provide a 12 volt output. As the alternator was attached to the end of the crankshaft, it was not anything like as easy to convert an older machine to this a.c. system. It was not a new idea for motorcycles, however: the ex-WD G3/L Matchless had originally been specified with an alternator, as had Bert Hopwood's 650cc BSA twin.

A fundamental change in engine design occurred during the mid-fifties, when unit-construction designs began to appear. There was no possibility of older machines being converted to follow suit, as the engine and gearbox became one combined unit, sharing the same crankcase casting. This, too, was not a new idea, as New Imperial, amongst others, had used it as far back as 1932. Triumph was the first major British manufacturer to adopt it after the war, when the Model 21 was launched in 1957 to commemorate 21 years having passed since Edward Turner's Speed Twin made its debut. That design established the vertical twin trend, one that continued with the new and more compact unit-construction twins.

One of the early casualties of the British motorcycle industry was Scott Motors (Saltaire) Ltd., who, early in 1950, announced it had gone into voluntary liquidation. The company had made just over 600 machines since the war which, being an expensive machine to purchase, meant not enough had been sold to keep the firm going. Fortunately, this old established company was not allowed to die completely and was bought by Matt Holder, of Aerco Jigs and Tools of Birmingham, where production was subsequently transferred. The Scott thereafter was built in very small numbers until, in July 1954, a 'modernised' version with pivoted fork rear suspension was announced.

Norton Motors was another company in financial difficulties, saved only by a takeover by Associated Motor Cycles Ltd., who made AJS and Matchless

Motorcycling in the 50s

An agreement with NSU, which led to Vincent selling the NSU-Vincent Fox and Lux, and NSU's Max models in the UK, failed to save the company from going into liquidation at the end of 1955. Note the crudely-added dualseat in place of the Fox's usual continental-style single saddle.

motorcycles. Made during February 1953, the Norton takeover startled the motorcycling world, especially when, in 1954, it was decided to cease production of the 16H and "Big Four" sidevalve models. There was no longer much demand for large capacity sidevalve models. The 596cc "Big Four" had the distinction of being the longest running of any production motorcycle, for it had been introduced in late 1909 as an ideal machine for sidecar use.

Norton production eventually transferred to Plumstead during the early sixties, after closure of its famous factory in Bracebridge Street, Birmingham. AMC had already acquired Francis Barnett in 1947, and James in 1951, although it allowed each company to retain its separate identity and an element of competitiveness. Later, however, AMC's influence became more evident when new models from all of the companies purchased began to incorporate components of obvious Plumstead origin, to look more alike. Fears about amalgamations within the industry had become a reality.

Sadly, one manufacturer which had to close it doors completely was Vincent Engineers (Stevenage) Ltd., the Vincent being another expensive motorcycle with a relatively small, but very enthusiastic clientele. Attempts in 1954 to diversify by making and selling a 48cc moped and developing a tenuous link with NSU to offer on the UK market three small capacity NSU-Vincents, all came to nothing. By the end of 1955, production finally came ceased.

Tandon Motors Ltd. of Watford had been formed in 1948 and, over the years, had made a name for itself with some very good lightweight two-strokes, both singles and twins, and even a competition model. Signs of impending financial problems became evident during the mid-fifties, but the company managed to keep going until May 1959, albeit with a reduced model range.

Although many new names appeared on the British motorcycle market, the majority of them related to either scooters or mopeds imported from the Continent. Their concessionaires established a sales and service organisation in this country, often under a completely different name from the make they sold. Apart from them, nine different makes of British motorcycle were an-

Few motorcycles have been made in Wales, even though production of the Bown began in north London under the Aberdale name. Well made, the Bown was short-lived as, by 1958, production in Tonypandy had ceased.

nounced during the '50s, of which only four continued in production for any reasonable amount of time. Of the others, some were little more than a brief announcement and a flitting appearance, disappearing almost as soon as they arrived.

Bond, the three-wheel car manufacturer based in Lancashire, produced an unorthodox-looking lightweight motorcycle in 1950. Powered by a 98cc Villiers engine with a two-speed gearbox, it had an all-alloy rigid frame, comprising a slanting, large section tapered oval tube from which the engine unit was suspended. A thin-looking undamped telescopic front fork provided the sole form of suspension. Both wheels - of the split rim type, shod with 4.00 x 16in tyres - were more than half covered by massively valanced mudguards. . Deep legshields straddled the engine on either side and there was a small carrier behind the spring saddle for carrying luggage. Lighting was direct, from the flywheel of the Villiers engine. A year later a de luxe version was announced, powered by a 125cc JAP two-stroke engine.

Although both machines were light in weight (the 98cc model weighed only 90lbs), sales were disappointing, and by the end of 1953 neither model remained in production. The Bond's unsightly appearance and lack of sophistication held little appeal. Perhaps it was as well, as the main frame tube had been rolled from alloy sheet and riveted, a potential source of long-term corrosion. A good many years later, someone riding one of these models through the Blackwall Tunnel had it break in half!

The Bown name appeared in 1950, initially on a 98cc autocycle that earlier had been marketed as the Aberdale by the same maker. It hailed from Wales, the manufacturer being the Bown Cycle Co. Ltd. of Tonypandy. A year later, a 98cc motorcycle was announced, with a two-speed gear. Both models were powered by a Villiers engine, the former with a single speed 2F unit and the latter with a 1F. Each was built along conventional lines. A third model was launched during mid-1952, powered by a 122cc Villiers engine with a three-speed gearbox. Despite all of the Bown range being well made and having a good reputation, production came to an end in 1954. There was a brief two-

The Brockhouse-made Indian was little short of a disaster and bore no relationship to its American-made predecessors. Few examples were sold in America, and even in Britain sales were minimal. The combination of a small capacity, underpowered sidevalve engine fitted with a three-speed gearbox and poor quality control sealed its fate.

Motorcycling in the 50s

Greeves, based near Southend in Essex, possessed an amazing amount of innovation for a small factory. Its 242cc Fleetwing and 325cc Fleetmaster twins, fitted with the rotary valve British Anzani engine, were particularly lively. A built-in Greeves 'trademark' was the alloy beam front down tube used in the frame construction.

DMW added a touch of colour to the otherwise drab British two-stroke scene, and experimented with frame tubes of square section. It may seem unusual for a motorcycle to have the name of a very popular model of car, but DMW had prior right to the Cortina name as Ford's car did not appear until 1962.

year revival in 1956 when Bown produced a pair of mopeds powered by a 47cc Sachs engine, but by 1958 production had ceased for good.

Many were surprised to see a motorcycle bearing the Indian name appear on the UK market, especially one made by a British manufacturer. The truth of the matter was that the once mighty Indian Motorcycle Company, of Springfield, Massachusetts, had, to all intents and purposes, ceased manufacture during the latter half of 1949 and, in its subsequent dismemberment, was split into two separate organisations. The Indian Sales Corporation, now ostensibly owned by Brockhouse Engineering of Southport, took on distribution throughout the USA of a number of British-made motorcycles, re-badged with the Indian name. Included amongst them was a new model, the Indian Brave, of their own design and manufacture. A far cry from the traditional Indian, it took the form of a 248cc sidevalve single built in-unit with a proprietary three-speed gearbox and foot-operated controls transposed to cater for the US market.

It first appeared in 1950, destined for export only, but made virtually no impact at all in a land where 'big is best'. Deliveries were diverted to the home market and here, too, the level of sales was far from impressive. Initially available with a rigid frame only, the Brave was supplemented by a plunger frame version in 1954, which met with a similar response. Quite apart from the fact that a 250cc side valve engine coupled to a three-speed gearbox is unlikely to provide exhilarating performance, both models were bedevilled by quality control problems. Production finally came to a close during 1955 and there were few who mourned the passing of the British-made Indian.

DMW of Dudley, Worcester, came into existence during 1950. Founded by 'Smoky' Dawson, the initials were a contraction of Dawson Motor Works. Interested only in making grass track bikes fitted with JAP engines, Dawson left when others in the company saw a better future in making lightweight two-strokes. That it was the correct decision there can be no doubt and DMW soon established its own niche, being unafraid to experiment with frames of square section tubing and pastel shade colour schemes. Competition models were included in the range for both trials and scrambles, and there were prospects at one time of a French AMC-engined road racer. DMW made its

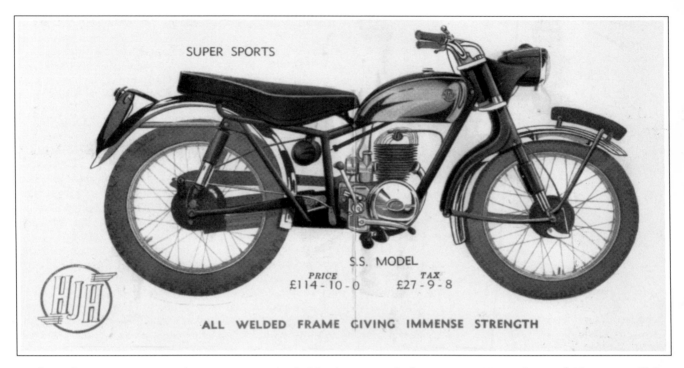

SUPER SPORTS

S.S. MODEL

PRICE £114-10-0   TAX £27-9-8

ALL WELDED FRAME GIVING IMMENSE STRENGTH

mark on the postwar two-stroke scene in a remarkably short period of time, both on and off road.

1951 became a milestone in the history of the British-made two-stroke, when the Greeves motorcycle came into existence. The brainchild of Bert Greeves, the founder of Invacar, who made invalid carriages at Thundersley, in Essex, the prototype featured an ingenious rubber in torsion suspension system. Built with competition use in mind, nothing much was heard about it for the next few years, although development continued. Ultimately, it resulted in this small company making a tremendous impact on competition events, elevating the two-stroke out of a life of drudgery, as related in a later chapter. It also produced some very fine road models, both singles and twins, all of them two-strokes.

A range of highly unorthodox lightweight two-strokes made its debut at the 1953 Earls Court Show, under the name of Commander. Made by the General Steel Group of Hayes, Middlesex, the design was so startlingly different from anything seen before it was difficult to make comparisons with contemporary design. Nonetheless, although the Commander never went into production it had sufficient merit for it to be included in the chapter that follows.

An old and once familiar name - that of Cotton - reappeared on the motorcycle scene in 1954. Although still made in Gloucester, the postwar company, E. Cotton (Motor Cycles) Ltd., was under totally different ownership and specialised only in Villiers-engined lightweights. Even so, the quality was still there, as was evident not only from the styling but also from the excellence of the paintwork. The marque retained its allegiance to competition work by having trials and scrambles models available and, later, a road racer. It was a welcome and long overdue return.

H.J. Hulsman of Glamorgan added another name to the list of Welsh motorcycle manufacturers when it began making the HJH in 1954 which ceased production after two years when the company went into liquidation. A great pity because the Super Sports model, with its Earles front fork, was particularly attractive and well-finished.

Motorcycling in the 50s

Another Welsh manufacturer commenced operations during 1954; H.J. Hulsman (Industries) of Neath, Glamorgan. Although the company remained in business for only a couple of years or so, it manufactured a small range of HJH single cylinder two-strokes built along conventional lines, powered by a Villiers engine. Also made was a small number of trials and scrambles models, similarly powered. Unfortunately, the concern ran into early financial problems and was declared bankrupt in 1956.

Once a well-known name of the '20s, Radco announced its intention of returning to motorcycle manufacture in 1954. The intended comeback was made with a 98cc lightweight two-stroke powered by a Villiers 4F two-speed engine unit. Built along conventional lines, the Radco 'Ace' differed from most other machines in one respect; it was fitted with a leading link front fork supplied by Metal Profiles. The prototype looked quite promising but, for reasons unknown, the reborn Radco never went into production. E.A. Radnall & Co. of Birmingham quietly withdrew and returned to making handlebars and similar accessories for the trade.

From the foregoing it will be seen that lightweight two-strokes were much in the ascendancy and offered a wide choice to the newcomer to motorcycling. A disturbing trend, though, was that the major four-stroke manufacturers had neglected the 250cc 'entry' market, with the exception of BSA, although Royal Enfield re-entered the market in 1954 and, in 1958, AMC. These moves were prompted by mounting pressure from the media to have a capacity limit introduced for provisional licence holders, especially at the 16 year old entry level.

The British motorcycle industry had, to its subsequent cost, as usual reacted too late to meet the demand for sporting and racing 250cc four strokes with which to counteract foreign competition. With imports from the Continent having increased alarmingly by the end of the decade, the writing was already on the wall.

Almost there

Traditionally, motorcyclists have been conservative in outlook and anything but receptive to change. Although new designs were often greeted with much enthusiasm and fervently discussed in reader's letters published by the motorcycling press, when it came to actual purchase it was usually a different story.

A classic example is that of the Douglas 'Endeavour'. When it was announced in 1934, the trade and the motorcycling press went into raptures over it. Their correspondence columns bristled with letters from intending purchasers, who sang its praises loudly. However, in the end only about 50 were made and sold ...

A similar situation occurred in 1946 when the new Sunbeam S7 twin made its debut. Graham Walker, then the editor of *Motor Cycling*, persuaded the legendary sprint racer, George Dance, to come out of retirement and be featured riding it, to add colour to the magazine's road test. An unorthodox model it certainly was, unlike anything George had ever ridden before. Yet although it was one of the first entirely new postwar designs to go into production, and the road test details were encouraging, it never sold in anything like the numbers expected.

It could be, of course, that prospective purchasers of any new design were reluctant to buy one of the early production models, when it was more than likely the manufacturer would need to make modifications in the light of user experience. It had long been recognised that the purchaser of any new design would, more likely than not, also fulfil the role of development tester. If anything went wrong, the machine went back to the dealer and was off the road until the problem had been resolved and modified replacement parts made available under guarantee (but fitted at the owner's expense). Be that as it may, new designs were essential if the industry was not to become sterile, assuming the requirements of the market had been correctly understood.

The fickleness of the would-be purchaser was not the only reason why

some promising new designs of the fifties failed to make headway, however. For a variety of reasons, not all of which were realised at the time, some models never got beyond the prototype stage. No one can deny that when John Wooler unveiled the machine that bore his name at the first postwar Motor Cycle Show in 1948 it represented a totally new approach to design. A 499cc horizontally-opposed four, it weighed only 210lb and required only two spanner sizes for dismantling and reassembly. The engine itself, built in unit with a four-speed gearbox, certainly struck new ground. The cylinders were arranged vertically, one above the other, necessitating the use of a rocking beam crankshaft assembly. The exhaust gases passed into a forward-mounted expansion chamber, before escaping through the lower frame tubes, whilst a cross tube in the duplex frame assembly - on which the footrests were mounted - concealed a tyre pump. A Wipac 'Genimag' magneto-generator driven by the crankshaft looked after the ignition and lighting, with a single Solex carburetter supplying the mixture. A sports version projected at the same time differed by having twin Amal carburetters and a dualseat in place of the traditional saddle.

The Wooler 'hallmark' lay in the design of the petrol tank, which extended forward of the steering head and had the headlamp mounted in its nose. A Wooler had been available before the 1914-18 war and even then their petrol tanks had been made along similar lines without the light unit. At one time they had used a yellow and black finish, so thereafter the Wooler was dubbed the 'Flying Banana'.

The front fork was also of Wooler's own design and quite unlike any other, having twin plunger-type suspension units at the extremity of each leg, one on each side of the front wheel spindle. Rear springing followed a similar layout, with twin plunger units each side of the frame to support the rear wheel. Final drive was by shaft to a spiral bevel. Production was claimed to be imminent and the retail prices were £254 (inclusive of Purchase Tax) for the standard model and £272.1s. for the sports model. These figures, however, were of little significance as the Wooler never went into production in this form. Nothing more was heard of it until the 1952 Motor Cycle Show, when it reappeared, with a totally different engine unit. Although the new 499cc Wooler still possessed some of its predecessor's unorthodox features, such as the elongated petrol tank and a plunger-type front fork assembly, the engine no longer had its pairs of cylinders one above the other. These had been rearranged side by side, so that a combination of forked and plain connecting rods could be used in place of the earlier and more complicated rocking beam arrangement. Exactly why this change was made is not clear, but some reports suggested that premature wear of the joints in the rocking beam arrangement had been the main reason. It was still possible to dismantle and reassemble the latest version using only two sizes of spanner and to remove the complete engine/ gear unit from the frame in ten minutes.

Other changes dispensed with the need for the exhaust gases to pass through the frame tubes, by using instead a two-into-one exhaust pipe on either side that terminated in a tapered silencer not unlike that of the prewar Triumph Tiger 100. Twin Solex carburetters supplied the mixture to each pair of cylinders. The suspension system had also been redesigned to use only single plunger-type units. Although light alloy was still used extensively in the machine's construction, its overall weight had increased significantly to 355lbs fully equipped. The price had crept up, too, from £254 to £292.4s.1d.

Production was again claimed to be imminent and there were hopeful signs when a Wooler was entered for the *Motor Cycling* Silverstone Saturday meeting in 1955. Ridden by Arnold Jones, it circulated at moderate speed, its suspension making a curious pattering sound. Perhaps deterred by its disappointing debut, the optimistic entry made for that year's Senior TT failed to materialise.

The Wooler was next seen at a Continental show in 1956 when further changes were evident. These related mainly to the frame, which had been completely redesigned to accommodate pivoted fork rear suspension, controlled by conventional hydraulically-damped suspension units. The exhaust was now fitted with barrel-type silencers and the mudguards were of different profile. Sadly, this appears to have been its swansong as nothing more was heard of it and Wooler's double-ended spanner motif was seen no more. This left one unanswered question: if such a highly unorthodox machine *had* appeared on the market, would its many novel features have compensated enough for its appearance to have made it a successful venture?

At the lower end of the market, where a low purchase price was more important than high performance, there was little incentive to make the humble two-stroke look particularly attractive. It did, after all, serve a basic function - as a means of commuting to and from work with good reliability and low running costs, or as a first purchase for the learner rider. It came as something of a surprise, therefore, that a complete newcomer to the lightweight two-stroke market was design conscious, and metaphorically grabbed the bull by its horns to launch three new and very unorthodox lightweight models at the 1952 Motor Cycle Show. They differed in nearly every respect from what the market had been accustomed to in the past and became the sensation of the show. The Commander had arrived.

Made by the General Steel Group of Hayes, Middlesex, and using a Villiers engine, the design was based on a beam-type frame from which the engine unit was suspended. Fabricated from welded square-section tubing, the beam had softly flowing lines, tapering almost to a point at its rearmost end, rather like an elongated letter 'S' lying on its side. The engine unit was carried in a loop that extended below the beam, enclosed within a detachable chrome-plated grille, referred to as a bonnet in the company's sales catalogue.

The front fork was of the leading link type, partially covered by an extensively valanced front mudguard and a fairing around the headstock. A stout rubber band on each side of the fork provided the undamped suspension medium. At the rear end, the pivoted fork suspension, also undamped, was controlled by a single compression spring. The swinging arm fork, made in square section tubing, was totally enclosed within a huge fairing attached to

At the 1954 Motor Cycle Show, John Wooler continued to give the impression that production of the machine bearing his name was imminent. By now its overall appearance had improved a little but, although it had many ingenious (and improved) design features, it is doubtful whether many would have bought it even though it drew the crowds at the show.

This racing Wooler made its debut during Motor Cycling's 1955 Silverstone Saturday meeting. Ridden by Arnold Jones it put up only a mediocre performance which would not have impressed the spectators.

3 revolutionary machines powered by *Villiers*

the Commander

modern low-cost motoring in armchair comfort

Was the Commander, in terms of styling, a case of too much, too soon, or did prospective purchasers see it as a sheep in wolf's clothing? Even today, nothing quite like it has been seen since.

the sub-frame, which also acted as the rear mudguard. It had provision for mounting the rear numberplate and rear lamp.

Even more controversial was the design of the headlamp, which was built into the fairing around the headstock; enclosed within a glass prism it had a triangular slotted grille above it. The handlebars passed through this grille, enclosed within a wing-like fairing, and had an inverted control lever in each end for the clutch and front brake. The whole effect was heightened by a two-tone metallic finish that emphasised the flowing lines of the frame.

Three models were available. The Commander 100 was a single gear autocycle, fitted with a 98cc Villiers 2F engine unit, which required a pedal-assisted start. Next came the Commander 200 Ultra-Lightweight, which dispensed with the need for pedals and was fitted with a 98cc Villiers 1F engine unit and an integral two-speed gearbox. The third model was the Commander 300 Lightweight, featuring a 122cc Villiers 10D engine unit and an integral three-speed gearbox. All three models were styled along identical lines and, as will be obvious, the model number code related to the number of gears.

As may be expected, such a highly unconventional design attracted a great deal of comment, with a touch of humour, too. Most comment centred around the grille enclosing the engine and a cartoon in *Motor Cycling* depicted a small boy pointing to it and asking a stand attendant "Does your parrot bite?". In no time at all, motorcyclists were referring to the Commander as the "Flying Toast-rack" or the "Flying Birdcage".

Was it too much, too soon? As in the case of the Wooler, no one will ever know. All three models vanished as quickly as they had appeared, so that, today, not one of the prototypes exists. From an economic viewpoint, they had been priced to compare favourably with their less attractive contemporaries, although their price structure may have been based on the assumption that they would sell in large numbers.

More to the point, perhaps, although the design itself was revolutionary, all that was being offered was three low-powered lightweights, which could hardly have justified the time and effort put into their cosmetic appeal. Yet, for all that, it was a bold attempt to lift the small capacity two-stroke from its usual drab environment and, as such, should be applauded. It was a landmark in the motorcycle market often emulated 15 years on.

The sidecar outfit was a familiar sight on Britain's roads during the early fifties. In the somewhat austere atmosphere that still prevailed long after the war had ended, the cost of the average car was well beyond the means of the family man, who instead used a sidecar outfit to go to and from work during the week and as a means of recreation for the family at weekends and the annual family holiday. Unfortunately, the choice of machine suitable for hauling an often heavily laden outfit was somewhat limited. Gone were the sidevalve vee-twins that were the weight haulers of the girder fork era: it boiled down to a choice between a BSA M20, M21 or M33, a Norton 16H or 'Big Four', a Panther Model 100 or sometimes a vertical twin. Only the decidedly better off could afford an Ariel Square Four or a Vincent Rapide.

Amongst the leading suppliers of sidecars was Watsonian Sidecars Ltd. of Birmingham. Ron Watson decided to investigate the possibility of making their own large capacity vee-twin especially for sidecar use, and opened discussions with J.A. Prestwich and Co., Ltd. of Tottenham, the famous engine manufacturers. A prototype design was completed and unveiled before the press during April 1951. Based on a 996cc sidevalve JAP vee-twin engine, it looked very impressive. Its existence had been a well-kept secret, although the more observant would have seen it on test around the Birmingham area.

Using a massive duplex tube frame, with plunger-type rear suspension, most of the space was filled by the engine, which had light alloy cylinder barrels with detachable cylinder heads. Engine oil was contained in a heavily finned oil tank of 1.5 gallon capacity fitted low down on the offside of the machine, between the rear of the gearbox and the rear suspension, for ease of access. Primary drive was by chain to a four-speed Burman gearbox, with chain final drive to the rear wheel. The front suspension was unusual - the fork being of the telescopic type - using rubber for the suspension medium. It was made by Dunlop.

As may be expected from a company so well versed in sidecar manufacture, every consideration had been given to what the sidecar driver most needed. The shapely petrol tank held no less than 5.5 gallons, in recognition that a sidevalve vee-twin is likely to be more thirsty than its ohv counterpart, but its load-lugging power was much more where it was needed. A large capacity battery was mounted behind the rear cylinder, and kept charged, via a rectifier, by an in-built alternator. Both brakes were of the twin leading shoe type, fully ventilated, cast in alloy with the hubs and having an inserted ferrous liner. It goes without saying that there was a four-point fixing for the attachment of a sidecar.

The complete machine was finished in mist green but, sadly, little performance data was available at the time of the launch other than the fact that the JAP engine developed 35bhp. Only the one prototype was made which, fortunately, has survived and can be seen in the National Motor Cycle Museum.

Various reasons have been put forward as to why the Watsonian never went into production, the most logical of which seems to be that JAP was unwilling to supply engines at an acceptable price in other than large numbers. The anticipated demand never materialised and, by the time the 1951 Motor Cycle Show came around towards the end of that year, all Watsonian had to show was its customary range of sidecars.

The other twin that might also have attracted sidecar drivers at the 1951 Motor Cycle Show was the 498cc Douglas twin. Ironically, it was shown attached to a single-seater Watsonian sidecar!

The cycle parts bore a close resemblance to those of the current production 348cc Mark V model, having torsion bar rear suspension and a Radiadraulic leading link front fork. A 'Plus'-type front brake outlined the need for improved braking, using the 'Plus' system of mudguard stays to replace the generally unsatisfactory arrangement used on the 348cc production models. The most

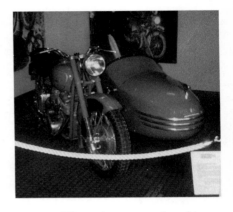

Ron Watson's prototype bore his company's name and was a bold attempt to bring back the big sidevalve vee-twin for serious sidecar work. It seems doubtful if JAP would have been able to supply these engines at an economic price unless guaranteed a sufficiently large number of orders. (Courtesy Mrs. Joyce Miller)

Motorcycling in the 50s

The 498cc Douglas twin - with virtually vibration-free engine and torsion bar rear suspension - would have offered the sidecar enthusiast another alternative. However, faced with one of many financial crises, the factory had no money available for its development so only the prototype was made, although some of the features were incorporated in the later 348cc Dragonfly model. (Courtesy E.F. Brockway)

The attachment of a single-seater Watsonian sidecar transformed the 498cc Douglas into a very attractive sidecar outfit, finished in a silvery green colour. (Courtesy E.F. Brockway)

obvious feature of the new, larger capacity model was an engine unit that seemed to occupy most of the space in the duplex tube frame.

Although the engine was similar in many respects to its smaller 348cc counterpart, a massive finned casting completely enclosed the Lucas Magdyno, mounted above the engine, and the air cleaner. Furthermore, the shape of the cylinder heads and rocker covers had been changed to give a more streamlined effect, being peardrop-shaped in profile. Both underslung exhaust pipes had a heavily finned clamp at the exhaust port. A welcome feature was an easily detachable oil filter unit at the base of the redesigned timing cover. Built in unit with the engine, and driven via a large diameter flywheel-type clutch, the gearbox, with chain final drive, appeared virtually unchanged to that used on the 350s.

Sidecar mounting lugs were evident, arranged so that a sidecar could be attached from either side to cater for overseas use. The whole outfit was finished in an attractive silvery green.

Although it was not evident, the Douglas company was in a parlous state financially. As a result, only the one prototype was made, with no money available for its further development. It, too, has survived, after being rescued and fully restored by a former managing director of the company. Not all of the design features were lost; the restyled cylinder heads and rocker covers appeared on the later 348cc 'Dragonfly' model, as did a modified enclosure over the latter's distributor and contact breaker points, on the top of the crankcase assembly.

If the majority of lightweight two-stroke manufacturers were reluctant to make any radical design changes, it seemed even more unlikely that those who manufactured autocycles would show any inclination at all to do so. The autocycle had not achieved anything like the measure of success anticipated just before World War 2, and sales were now on the decline.

However, Frank Rainbow of Weston-Super-Mare had other ideas. A design and development engineer, he considered it was time to show there was room for improvement in autocycle design too. Convinced the autocycle did not form a sufficiently strong link between the bicycle and the motorcycle, as its originator had intended, he set about proving his point.

The Rainbow was startlingly different, giving a first impression of a modern penny farthing through the use of different size wheels. Whilst its overall appearance was distinctly odd, the design bristled with a host of ingenious ideas, worthy of further description. The frame was of the 'open' or 'step-thru' type, having no top tube. Two tubes ran downwards from the webbed and welded headstock assembly to pass under the engine/gear unit, before sweeping upwards to form the rear wheel fork. Cross tubes were welded between them at intervals, there being a complete absence of a saddle tube or chainstays. In their place, a welded-on pillar, rising from each main tube, carried an adjustable cantilever bracket that supported a Dunlopillo single seat pad.

The front fork was of the single blade bicycle type, attached by links to a central stem, its movement controlled by rubber bands. A cantilever bracket carried a 5.5 inch diameter headlamp, so that it was not affected by the movement of the fork. A 98cc Villiers 1F two-speed engine/gear unit provided the motive power, its upper portion fully enclosed within a domed, pressed steel cover, sprung into position over rubber blocks. A choke lever protruded through a slot cut in its upper surface. At a quick glance, it appeared as though the engine had two flywheel magnetos, but the circular 'drum' on the nearside was a silencer without any baffles. It had been constructed so that the exhaust gases swirled around until they had lost their momentum and could be discharged via a short tail pipe with a perforated inner end. Fuel was contained in a circular 6 pint petrol tank mounted across the top of the twin frame tubes, just below the handlebars.

Many of Frank Rainbow's original design features were included in the Rainbow Sprite, in which Swallow showed an interest. No longer with wheels of unequal diameter, its overall appeal was improved and in some respects it anticipated the lightweight runabouts that became so popular in later years. (Courtesy R. Cordon Champ)

The front wheel was of 26 inch diameter, carrying an 1.5 inch section tyre. The rear wheel was only 20 inches in diameter, carrying a 2.5 inch section tyre. Both had hub brakes. The reason for the smaller diameter rear wheel was to enable a low riding position. It was quickly detachable and had provision for easily disengaging the rear brake torque arm. The mudguards were rigidly mounted and offered ample weather protection, aided by leg shields attached to the front of the frame tubes. Gear changing was accomplished by a simple trigger arrangement on the handlebars, like that of the James Comet.

A road test published in *Motor Cycling* during 1950 was very complimentary and showed the Rainbow was capable of just over 40mph on

Motorcycling in the 50s

the level. It could climb a hill of 1 in 4 without difficulty, and would pull almost down to walking speed. Quiet in use, and easy to handle in a confined space, it tipped the scales at only 112lb.

The Rainbow was yet another intriguing prototype that never went into production. Swallow had shown some interest as Frank Rainbow had designed that company's Gadabout scooter, described in Chapter Six, but came to the conclusion that its odd appearance would be a deterrent to sales. Instead, Rainbow produced a modified design for Swallow, the Sprite, with equal size wheels. It never went into production either, although the prototype has survived. It was last seen on the Vintage MCC's stand at one of the Classic Bike shows held at Stafford.

Many prototype designs have been produced by the British motorcycle industry over the years, but most were kept under wraps and rarely, if ever, seen by other than privileged factory personnel. Occasionally, parts of them have surfaced, often when a manufacturer has ceased business and the premises are being cleared out or demolished. Even so, it is rare for a complete machine to have survived, as most were scrapped.

Home-designed and built racing specials sometimes showed surprising results, none more so than Bob Geeson's R.E.G. 250cc dohc vertical twin. It was ridden with success on short circuits by riders such as John Surtees and Derek Minter, whilst its best performance in the Isle of Man achieved 10th in the 1953 Lightweight TT. Here it is seen in action at the Crystal Palace ridden by John Surtees. (Courtesy Castrol (UK) Ltd.)

New designs were not always the province of the established manufacturer, however. Quite often, well thought-out ideas would come from private individuals with an inventive mind, and many quite remarkable machines have been produced with limited resources in backyard sheds. Sadly, there is the world of difference between making a one-off and getting it into limited production, with all the attendant problems. This is probably why so many other promising new designs foundered at the prototype stage; practicality had been over-ridden by enthusiasm.

Taking the effort out of cycling

A market for some form of mechanical attachment that would take the physical effort out of pedalling a bicycle has been with us for a long time. One of the earliest designs was the 'outrigger' Wall Autowheel, first manufactured in 1909. A small capacity (119cc) two-stroke engine mounted on a sprung tubular chassis with its own 'third' wheel gear-driven by the engine, it was clamped by struts to the offside of a bicycle, in close proximity to the rear wheel. It added about 40lb in weight and was capable of propelling a rider on a bicycle at an average of 25mph on the level, on a reasonably smooth surface. The Autowheel was one of several such devices, all of which could be purchased for between £12 and £18.

Variations on this theme - some of them a cross between a bicycle and a motorcycle - were frequently popular. The latter variety had the engine mounted in a specially-made frame, with a spring front fork assembly more robust than that of the average bicycle, and wheels with better brakes. It was this approach that eventually led to the introduction of the autocycle during the late thirties, a definition of which is given in the first edition of the Iliffe book *Your Autocycle*, published during 1949. It reads "a machine on the lines of a bicycle, with pedals, pedalling gear and an engine not exceeding, in size, 100cc".

For a brief spell immediately before and after World War 2, the autocycle became quite popular, despite its limitations in having only a clutch and no gearbox. Local authorities often equipped district nurses and midwives with them. The weekly magazine *Motor Cycling* tried to encourage the use of the name Wilfred to describe them, a name derived from a very popular cartoon in the *Daily Mirror* - Pip, Squeak and Wilfred. Motorcyclists tended to regard the autocycle as a 'pipsqueak' and often referred to it as such, on account of its small capacity but, despite that, Wilfred or Pipsqueak were names that never caught on.

Although an autocycle was cheap to run at a penny a mile and would average up to 140mpg, its pedals had to be used when hills were encoun-

The 98cc autocycle was very popular before and after the war and cost a penny a mile to run. Many local authorities bought them for employees to use and they were quite often seen ridden by midwives and district nurses. The dropped frame made them suitable for use by either sex, but as they had only a single gear with a countershaft, those pedals were needed to give 'light pedal assistance', as the advertisements put it, on hills.

Motorcycling in the 50s

The French-made 45cc VeloSolex, a complete, purpose-built machine, was the forerunner of the moped. Vast numbers were made and production continued for over four decades. This was a highly successful design that heralded the transformation of the cyclemotor attachment into the far more satisfactory moped. (Courtesy R. Cordon Champ)

tered, for what was optimistically termed light pedal assistance. Without a gearbox, the engine of a two-stroke of under 100cc has limited torque. As an autocycle was a complete and specially-made machine, it was a somewhat costly acquisition at around the £70 mark, beyond the means of many cyclists. Their salvation came when motorised attachments began to appear on the market at the end of the forties and during the early fifties. These could be fitted to their already owned bicycle. They cost, on average, about £25, and were free from Purchase Tax. Those who lived on the Continent had already taken advantage of this new generation of cyclemotors, especially in France, Germany and Italy.

Motor Cycling published a survey of the situation in France in its 23rd February 1950 issue. It found that there was between 130,000 and 140,000 cyclemotors of under 50cc capacity in use by the 22 million inhabitants of the Republic. The most popular of ten designs highlighted was the 45cc VeloSolex. To put matters in their correct perspective, however, it should be explained that no road tax was payable in France, nor was there any need for registration or insurance if the engine capacity was below 50cc. A strange anomaly was that a pedal-powered bicycle owner in France had to pay an annual duty of 120 francs (25p at that time), but when the bicycle was fitted with a cyclemotor, it was free of duty! Instead, fuel tax had to be paid on the amount of petrol used, which did not amount to much in view of the small amount (say 230mpg) consumed by such a tiny engine.

Here it should be said that only for convenience was the VeloSolex regarded as a cyclemotor, on account of its 45cc engine capacity. In point of fact, it was neither a cyclemotor or an autocycle. First manufactured during 1945, and continuing in production for a very long time with virtually no significant changes in specification, it was the forerunner of what today is regarded as a moped. Sold as a complete powered bicycle with a 'U' type open frame that made it suitable for use by both sexes, over 17,000 had been made and sold in France during the first half of 1949, against a total output of 27,000 cyclemotors during the same period. By 1950, VeloSolex production was running at 150 a day and it was alleged something like 70,000 had been made since production commenced four years earlier.

The VeloSolex was unusual in a number of respects, even though it was fitted with a conventional two-stroke engine. The carburetter was floatless, relying on a membrane pump attached to the front of the crankcase to draw fuel from the circular fuel tank mounted vertically on the offside of the engine. The membrane was activated by changes in crankcase pressure, which caused it to pulsate, a 'spill' catchment returning excess fuel to the fuel tank. Another unusual feature was the use of two trigger handlebar levers. The longer of the two operated the decompressor when pushed right, against the handlebars, and gave full throttle when pushed fully to the left. In mid-position it restricted the speed to about 16mph. The shorter lever acted as a 'stay' to retain the longer lever in its partially open setting.

There was potential for cyclemotors in the UK, despite the need for the owner to hold a driving licence, have insurance cover and pay road tax after the unit had been fitted, the bicycle registered and the front and rear number-

plates attached. By 1950, the VeloSolex became available in the UK, along with several cyclemotors of the 'clip-on' type.

Drive methods varied. The VeloSolex was driven by the front wheel via an emery-faced roller that pressed on the periphery of the tyre. Other engines, designed by their makers to be mounted behind the saddle, used a similar method of friction drive to the rear wheel. In either case, the drive roller could be raised or lowered, so that, if need be, the bicycle could be ridden in the normal manner.

The British Cyclemaster was an early design that showed great ingenuity. It was manufactured by Electrical and Musical Industries of Hayes, Middlesex, a company more famous for its gramophone records sold under the 'His Master's Voice' label. It was HMV who took over Rudge in

1935 when the Coventry-based motorcycle manufacturer went bankrupt. This meant HMV had previous experience of manufacturing not only complete motorcycles and engines, but also autocycles. Its creation was a reincarnation of the Singer Motor Wheel, patented as early as 1899.

Built into a wheel which could be substituted for the original rear wheel of an adult bicycle, the Cyclemaster's tiny, single cylinder two-stroke engine had a capacity of 25.7cc (later increased to 32cc). The engine featured a rotary inlet valve and drove a cork-lined clutch by an endless chain. Another endless chain transferred the drive to a sprocket riveted to the inside of the casing. Everything, including the fuel tank, was housed within an enlarged hub like a saucepan lid which was 13 inches in diameter and open on the nearside. The complete assembly added only 20lbs in weight when fitted to a bicycle and was capable of sustaining a speed of up to 20mph. The Cyclemaster could be supplied and fitted for a modest £55. It was robust and required little maintenance.

Although ingenious, the 32cc Cyclemaster was a reincarnation of the Singer Motor Wheel patented in 1899. The capacity of the engine was, of necessity, somewhat small, but the Cyclemaster's greatest advantage was the ease with which it could be fitted to a pedal cycle in place of the original rear wheel.
(Courtesy Tony Brown.)

Motorcycling in the 50s

The Cyclaid was a variation of a name (Cycklaid) that the Sheppee Motor Co. Ltd. of York used for a front wheel pedal cycle attachment it made from 1919 to 1926. The Cyclaid was unusual in having belt drive to a pulley attached to the rear wheel's spokes, enabling smoother transmission as the belt served also as a shock absorber.

The 49cc Mini Motor, with its emery-faced roller drive to the rear tyre, was probably the best selling of the British-made designs. It was easy to fit, although a section of the rear mudguard had to be cut away to allow the roller to press on the tyre. The drive could be disengaged to allow the pedal cycle to be ridden in the normal way. (Courtesy Tony Brown.)

The Cymota was an early British front wheel drive design. Enclosed within a bonnet with ventilation louvres, the 45cc two-stroke engine was of conventional three port design, transmitting the drive direct to the front wheel by a carborundum-faced roller. The roller could be raised clear of the tyre so that the bicycle could be ridden in the usual manner. A single lever control on the handlebars acted as the throttle, and also operated a decompressor to aid starting. The Cymota scored against its contemporaries by having its own built-in direct lighting equipment, the headlamp being mounted in the all-enclosing bonnet. Made by Components (Birmingham) Ltd., the Cymota was distributed by Blue Star Garages and retailed at £18.18s.

The 31cc Cyclaid (re-using an old and forgotten name of the past) offered yet another type of drive by using a vee belt to transmit the final drive to a large diameter pulley clamped to the rear wheel spokes. The engine was mounted above the wheel, attached to the saddle pillar via Silentbloc rubber bushes. A countershaft driven by helically cut gears permitted the drive to be disengaged. The controls amounted to a twist grip throttle and a decompressor. More expensive to purchase, the Cyclaid cost £24. Although a belt provides a much softer drive than a chain, it suffers the disadvantage of a tendency to slip when wet. The complete answer could, of course, have been to use a toothed belt, but these had yet to be invented ...

Of all the cyclemotors in use, the Mini Motor seemed the most popular. Another rear-mounted design, it was located above the rear wheel and drove a carborundum roller that bore on the tyre through a cutaway in the rear mudguard. Of 49.9cc, it attached to the saddle pillar and was a very compact and tidy-looking unit, with its blue-painted fuel tank mounted immediately above the horizontal single cylinder two-stroke engine. Sold by Mini Motor (Great Britain) Ltd. of Croydon, Surrey, it cost £21 and wore out tyres at an alarming rate.

Soon, there were so many different makes of cyclemotor on the market that the potential purchaser had an almost infinite choice of engine position, method of drive and how the engine itself was mounted. For those who desired the ultimate and were not price conscious, the answer lay in the Italian-made Ducati Cucciolo. This boasted a 48cc overhead valve engine fitted with an integral two-speed gear, carried low down, in front of the bottom bracket. Imported and sold by Britax Ltd. for £40, it carried a six month guarantee and, with all its fittings, added only 7.5lbs in weight. Some claimed it was capable of 40mph at 100mpg.

Although the British motorcycle industry welcomed any attempt to get newcomers onto two wheeled transport propelled by an internal combustion engine, it went to great lengths to ensure that those who rode bicycles fitted with cyclemotors were not classified as motorcyclists, nor their machines considered to be miniature motorcycles.

Up to a point, this viewpoint was acceptable, as the majority of those

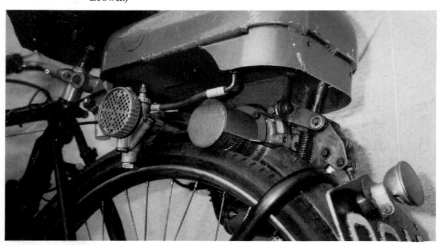

Taking the effort out of cycling

who purchased a cyclemotor did so only as a means to an end - to take the effort out of pedalling at relatively low cost and avoid the frequent public transport strikes. Few would have seriously considered buying a conventional motorcycle. The motorcycling press was in accord with this and did not include cyclemotors in its annual buyer's guides, although it did still report on new designs.

Tyres presented cyclemotorists with problems: if a novice rider tended to raise and lower a roller drive to act as an alternative to a clutch, chunks were ripped from a tyre designed for road contact only. With care, a bicycle tyre used with a roller drive could be expected to last for 2000 miles. Tread patterns were of importance, too, as block or knobbly tread tyres suffered most when they came into sudden contact with a fast revolving roller. Tyres were soon designed and made for use in conjunction with a cyclemotor roller drive, with life expectancy greatly extended. Accordingly, these were more expensive..

Statistics showed 12 million of the UK's population rode bicycles in 1950, which highlighted the opportunity of increasing cyclemotor sales. Unfortunately, the prospective UK purchaser was always at a disadvantage, compared to his or her counterpart on the Continent, as it was necessary to have a licence and register the machine before venturing on the road with a bicycle fitted with a cyclemotor. At that time, a provisional driving licence cost 5s (25p) and it was necessary to carry 'L' plates and to pass a driving test before a motorcycle (Class G) licence could be taken out. The annual road tax on a cyclemotor was 17s.6d. (87.5p) and insurance cover would cost from 12s.6d (62.5p) to £2, depending on the type of cover required. Whilst not an outright deterrent, the extra outlay represented something like a 15%

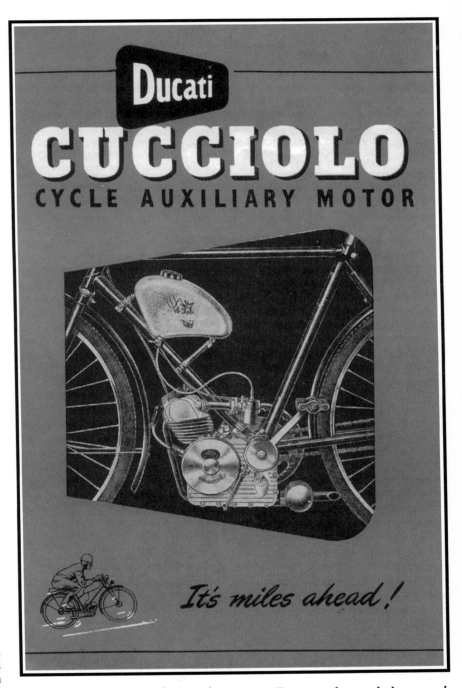

The 48cc Ducati Cucciolo (little pup) was very well engineered, as might be expected. It weighed only 17.5lbs, would return over 250mpg under favourable conditions and permit the pedal cycle to which it was fitted to cruise at 25-30mph. It retailed through Britax at 18 guineas (£18.90p).

Motorcycling in the 50s

addition to the cost of the cyclemotor, which had to be taken into account.

A most unorthodox design, seen in 1952, was the diminutive 18cc Lohmann, a bottom bracket attachment that drove the rear wheel by roller. This is worthy of special mention because its tiny two-stroke engine was of the compression-ignition type, having neither a carburetter or an ignition system. The right-hand twist grip controlled the fuel supply and the left-hand twist grip the compression ratio and port timing. Of German origin, it was imported by Britax (London) Ltd., who seemed to have an liking for importing the unusual. Priced at £25.4s, it was anything but a success and vanished within a season. Quite apart from its small capacity engine (which, it was claimed, would sustain a speed of 15mph), it took dexterity and understanding to manipulate the controls and get it to run satisfactorily for more than 50 yards!

Undoubtedly the most ingenious of all the cyclemotor designs was the Power Wheel, which was the brainchild of Cyril Pullin, winner of the 1914 TT and a brilliant engineer. The Power Wheel was a unit enclosed within the rear wheel but, in Pullin's design, the 39.9cc two-stroke engine was of the rotary type, revolving around a stationary crankshaft that also served as the wheel's spindle. The Power Wheel bristled with novel features that included a rotary induction valve, magneto ignition, a gear-driven alternator for lighting and a five plate clutch. There was even sufficient room to include a 7 inch diameter expanding brake! To be made by Tube Investments Ltd. of Birmingham, the prototype seemed certain of success, yet it failed to get into production. Sheer complexity resulted in proportionally high production costs, which would have had to be passed on to the customer in such a competitive market. In addition, it may have arrived on the scene just too late as, by 1953, the cyclemotor was beginning to decline in popularity, superseded by the up-and-coming, purpose-designed moped.

The moped clearly had advantages over the cyclemotor, even if it was more expensive. The addition of a cyclemotor to the average bicycle meant the latter would have to travel at speeds much greater than ever intended in its original form. An unsprung front fork let the rider take all the road shocks whilst the block brakes which, at best, were barely able to stop a cycle reasonably quickly in an emergency, possessed little stopping power at all in the wet. Overall cost seemed to be about the only advantage in a cyclemotor's favour. The VeloSolex and, later, the Mobylette, two of the most successful of all mopeds, emphasised the superiority of the purpose-designed machine. A moped took care of all the problems the power-assisted cyclist was having to face.

Surprisingly, BSA did not enter the cyclemotor market until as late as early 1953, when it introduced the 35cc Winged Wheel model, another engine in the rear wheel design which enjoyed a moderate run of success. Even so, by the time that year's Motor Cycle Show came around BSA, like Cyclemaster, played it safe by having a moped on display as well, a relatively easy achievement for BSA, as it made quality bicycles in considerable numbers and could supply a Webb spring front fork and a Winged Wheel model for £43.9s.6d. Cyclemaster did more or less the same, but had to use a bicycle made by Norman Cycles of Ashford, Kent. Cyclemaster took the 32cc engine out of its rear wheel and clamped it to the lower down tube of the bicycle. It then drove by chain, the complete machine costing £44. Neither machine, of course, was a moped in the true sense, though each represented a form of developing compromise.

SUPER

The French-made Mobylette was available in a number of versions and was one of the most popular mopeds in the UK, partly due to its simple but ingenious automatic transmission. Purchase was simple through Pride and Clarke's easy terms; initially it was imported by Pride and Clarke's own import agency.

A late newcomer to the UK moped market, in 1955, was the Mobylette, made by Motobecane in Paris. A true moped, the De Luxe version had a simple but very effective method of automatic transmission. The primary drive used a vee belt and pulley arrangement, one pulley of which expanded centrifugally to act as a clutch. When the engine was idling, the pulley was open and the belt ran slack, so there was no drive, but as the throttle was opened, the engine speed increased and the pulley flanges closed up, causing the belt to run higher up and take up the slack. As a result, the machine began to move forward as engine power was taken up. Final drive was by rear chain in the conventional manner.

The Mobylette range sold well and was marketed by Motor Imports Co. Ltd. of London SW9, the import agency within the Pride and Clarke organisation. The standard model sold for £49.16s and the De Luxe version

"No effort at all"

Add POWER to your cycle

simply fix a

VINCENT

Firefly

ALL-WEATHER

CYCLE MOTOR

– and journey with ease

Vincent enthusiasts would never acknowledge the 48cc Firefly cycle attachment: it was as if it never existed. The design originated from H. Miller and Co., the one-time Birmingham motorcycle electrical equipment manufacturer.

Motorcycling in the 50s

The German-made 49cc NSU Quickly moped was arguably the best of all the mopeds and very highly rated. A Cavallino sports version became available in the UK during late 1958, fitted with a three- speed gearbox and telescopic front fork. The alloy cylinder barrel of all the Quickly models featured a new departure; a chrome-plated bore that dispensed with the need for a liner.

for £52.12s. A third and even more sophisticated version, the Mobymatic, featured a clutch and a three-speed gear that was fully automatic. It sold for £89.15s.7d.

Also of Continental origin, and what many regarded as the best moped of all, was the German-made NSU Quickly. This had a pressed steel beam-type frame from which a single cylinder two-stroke engine was slung. With an alloy cylinder barrel and head and a chromium-plated cylinder bore, the engine was built in unit with a handlebar controlled two-speed gearbox. Final drive was by chain, which also linked up with the pedals. A pressed steel front fork was of the leading link type and both wheels were a bicycle-sized 26 inches in diameter. The specification of this stylish and well finished machine included a Continental-type pivoted single pillar saddle, a centre stand, knock-out wheel spindles and a rear carrier. Expensive by some standards, it sold surprisingly well at £59.18s. and was marketed initially by Vincent Engineers (Stevenage) Ltd., who had a short term liaison with NSU and acted as UK distributor until NSU set up its own UK-based operation.

The transition point had now been reached. With the superiority of the moped now evident, at the 1955 Motor Cycle Show there were no less than 21 different makes of moped on the market but only 9 cyclemotors. A handful of diehard cyclemotor manufacturers managed to hang on until the bitter end, although BSA decided it best to fade gracefully from the scene. All it had to offer that was new was a cross between a moped and a scooter, as mentioned in the following chapter.

Although the British motorcycle industry had been anxious to keep at arm's length all clip-on cyclemotor type of attachments, it began to appreciate the 'numbers game' with the emergence of the moped. Although the moped fulfilled only a basic role, it was a complete purpose-built machine with purchase price and running costs at affordable levels.

Official recognition for this new concept of two wheeled power had, surprisingly, come from the staid Auto-Cycle Union. In 1952, the AC-U found there was sufficient interest in cyclemotors for it to persuade the British Two Stroke Club to organise a demonstration trial. Starting and finishing at Wembley Stadium, the riders followed a 20 mile road section, which included a test hill off the Watford by-pass. It attracted 56 contestants on a variety of different makes, 15 of which qualified for a First Class Award. The need to maintain an average speed of 12mph in inclement weather revealed some of the machines' shortcomings. Other competitive events then allowed mopeds. Long term, it made it easier for the industry to accept the moped as an ultra-lightweight motorcycle which, after it replaced the cyclemotor, was around for the next thirty years.

By 1956 the moped market had blossomed, with so many different marques and models in the UK market that it became difficult to keep track of them. A real consumer problem, however, not obvious at the time of purchase, was that there was no guarantee how long some of the models would remain in production, for those of Continental origin often were brought in as single waggon loads only. This not only affected the supply of spare parts, but also eventual re-sale value.

The later newcomers were Continental in origin, some of them previously unknown in the U.K. In 1957, Maserati, the illustrious Italian car manufacturer, using a factory made redundant by an era that could not afford its cars, exported to Britain a 49cc moped with a three-speed engine/gear unit, telescopic front fork and pivoted fork rear suspension. A couple of months later, MV Agusta followed suit. MV's 48cc Ciclomotore had a Maserati-like specification, apart from plunger-type rear suspension. Both Italian machines had a relatively short sales life and disappeared from the market within a year. Bearing prestige names, they were always at a price disadvantage, quite apart from the fact that the Italians found they could sell all they could make in their home market.

Amazingly, five remaining cyclemotor manufacturers were still exhibiting their now outmoded clip-on attachments at the 1958 Motor Cycle Show. Having only price advantages in their favour, it seems remarkable that the Teagle managed to hold on for so long with minimal sales.

Moped sales continued at a high level for two more decades, encouraged later by favourable changes in legislation that restricted 16 year old learners to a 50cc machine for their first year on the road. Later still, the need for a moped to be fitted with pedals (an essential part of its UK definition) was rescinded, although the engine had then to be restricted to ensure its maximum speed would not exceed 30mph. Sales increased to a peak of 90,917 in 1981, after which they began to fall off dramatically. It had been a good business that provided mass transport economically for many.

During recent years, there has been a small resurgence of interest in cyclemotors amongst members of the Vintage MCC. This has been sufficient to allow a separate Cyclemotor Section of the Club to be formed to encourage the preservation and use of these attachments made some 40 or so years ago, and to organise a 100 mile annual run for them. All the old names are there, unlike those of many of the much bulkier motorcycles which were often sent for scrap. A rare cyclemotor or moped does still sometimes surface after many years at the back of a garden shed ...

There was always an alternative method of powering a pedal cycle without having to use an internal combustion engine. Lucas carried out feasibility studies using battery-power, one example of which was borrowed by Yehudi Menuhin, the violinist. An electric vehicle enthusiast of long-standing he would have fully appreciated the fact that the cycle did not contribute to atmospheric pollution. (Courtesy Lucas Industries plc)

The scooter boom

The early origins of the scooter are somewhat obscure, giving rise to a widespread belief that the concept originated in Italy. In point of fact, nothing could be further from the truth, as the scooter was a British invention conceived well before the 1914-18 war, when it enjoyed a brief spell of interest, more as a novelty than a serious means of transport. Some examples had no seat so that the rider stood as on a child's scooter, suggesting that they were used as little more than a short distance runabout. Of those that had a seat, the commercial version of the ABC Scootamota had a large cupboard-like box below it, for carrying parcels, whilst the Oriental model had a fringed canopy above the seat to protect the rider's head from the sun!

The first of an entirely new generation of designs to make any real impact on the postwar UK market were both of Italian origin: the Lambretta, made by Innocenti of Milan, and the Vespa, made by Piaggio at its Pontedera plant. The latter was the first to make its debut in the UK, at the 1949 Motor Cycle Show.

The way in which the scooter achieved almost instant acceptance in Europe's industrial centres had not escaped the attention of Claude McCormack. He had been appointed manager of Douglas (Kingswood) Ltd. by the Westminster Bank, after Douglas had run into another of its many financial crises and the Official Receiver was brought in. Visualising a golden opportunity to increase revenue by adding a scooter to the Douglas range of motorcycles, McCormack negotiated a licensing agreement with Piaggio. The Douglas works in Kingswood, Bristol, had both the production space and the facilities and skill for Vespa manufacture. As a result, on 15th March 1951, the first Bristol-made Vespa was launched at the works, well in advance of its intended debut at the Earls Court Show. McCormack had made a shrewd and profitable move: even if the dyed-in-the-wool Douglas motorcycle enthusiast refused to acknowledge the Vespa's existence, the company's dealers were delighted to stock and sell the new two-wheeler.

Although the Lambretta made its UK debut several years later, *Motor Cy-*

cling had road tested an early import from Germany during mid-1949, where they were being made under licence by NSU. Of independent design and manufacture, both the small wheeled Lambretta and the Vespa were powered by their manufacturer's own 125cc single cylinder two-stroke engine and integral handlebar control-operated three-speed gearbox, mounted in close proximity to the rear wheel. Initially, the Lambretta had an air-cooled engine, a 'U' type frame that offered little weather protection and no rear suspension. The Vespa, on the other hand, had an enclosed fan-cooled engine, single-sided pivoted fork rear suspension and all-enveloping bodywork of pressed steel monocoque construction. By 1951, and after substantial redesign, Lambretta adopted a layout similar to that of the Vespa. Both now had a handlebar high front apron which, when fitted with a perspex screen, afforded the rider reasonable weather protection without a motorcyclist's protective clothing. Quickly detachable 8 inch diameter interchangeable wheels, with provision for carrying a spare, meant a puncture posed a problem.

Finished in a distinctive polychromatic green, the Vespa had a distinguishing feature that subsequently became its hallmark - a pronounced bulge either side of the rear wheel. The detachable cover on the right provided access to the engine unit, whilst the fixed one on the left had an opening flap to provide access to a locker that contained the battery and toolkit.

The British-made Vespa differed only in minor detail to its Italian-made counterpart, the most noticeable of which was the headlamp mounting. On the Italian-made model, this was built into the top of the front mudguard but its low height contravened the UK vehicle lighting regulations. Instead, it had to be repositioned at

Douglas was not able to make an exact copy of the original Italian-made Vespa as the low mounted headlamp on the front mudguard contravened UK lighting regulations. (Courtesy E.F. Brockway)

The problem was overcome by relocating the headlamp at the top of the front apron, although this meant that it no longer turned with the front wheel. (Courtesy E.F. Brockway)

The Lambretta, although styled along similar lines to those of the Vespa, had its own distinctive bodywork. A later LD version is illustrated, with rear-mounted spare wheel and separate continental-style seats.

the top of the apron, where it could no longer turn in unison with the front wheel. A large capacity shopping basket could now be hung from a hook to occupy the free space available above the front mudguard. Manufacturer's optional extras included the aforementioned Perspex windscreen and a spare wheel and tyre with an extra fuel container set in its centre. Only the so-called 'Rod Model' was available at the time of the launch, taking its name from the rod and universal joint mechanism used to operate the three-speed gearbox from the left-hand handlebar twistgrip. The Vespa was competitively priced at £149.16s.5d., inclusive of speedometer (still a mandatory extra on some motorcycles) and Purchase Tax.

When the Lambretta was launched in the UK, two versions were available: the LC model (which had a fully-enclosed side panel engine) and the Model C, whose 'works' were open to display under the saddle. The LC model retailed at £177.10s, inclusive of speedometer and Purchase Tax, with the former listed as an 'extra', even though it was a statutory requirement. The model with less bodywork, the Model C, was priced at £152.10s inclusive. The importer was the British-Italian Trading Co. Ltd., of 75, Bishopsgate, London, EC2.

One British manufacturer had not remained idle when it came to scooter design and manufacture. The Swallow Gadabout, made by the Swallow Coachbuilding Co. Ltd. of Walsall, had displayed its own commercial scooter outfit at the first postwar Motor Cycle Show in 1948. Permanently attached to an all-metal, box-type sidecar with a carrying capacity of 11 cu ft, the Gadabout had its good points, although styling was not one of them. Initially its balloon tyres were expected to obviate the need for any suspension, but later models had a leading link front fork, its movement controlled by a rubber in torsion assembly similar to that used in the company's sidecars. A 122cc Villiers engine was located under the Gadabout's seat, with ducted fan cooling. Detachable panels allowed access. The disc-type wheel sizes were 4.00 x 8in. The outfit retailed at £115, inclusive of Purchase Tax, and a year later the Gadabout could be supplied in solo form, with a number of improvements, for an inclusive cost of £103.1s.1d.

The Gadabout never offered Lambretta or Vespa a serious challenge, and few were seen on the road. Not only did the Villiers engine have a performance well inferior to that of its Italian counterparts, also the scooter itself so obviously lacked visual appeal. It was not listed at the 1951 Motor Cycle Show.

Controversy arose frequently about the small diameter of a scooter's wheels, which did not seem able to provide road-going stability. It is an established scientific fact that the larger the diameter of a spinning wheel, the less easily it can be deflected from its path, due to the gyroscopic effect. Even so, Vespa and Lambretta owners seemed content with small diameter wheels and tyres of advanced design for there were few complaints. Nonetheless, several scooter manufacturers were in favour of increasing wheel size to achieve better stability. Italy's Moto Guzzi fitted 17 inch diameter wheels to its 192cc Galletto scooter, alleged to be one of the best to handle scooters made.

Motor Cycling published a road test of the 192cc Galletto in its 13th January 1955 issue. Apart from having interchangeable wheels and carrying a spare on its front apron, this model also had a leading link front fork, pivoted fork rear suspension and, on later versions, a 6 volt electric starter. The tester described it as a highly successful marriage of the best points in scooter and motorcycle practice, to which the traditional Moto Guzzi horizontal ohv engine

and gearbox layout lent itself so admirably. Top speed was about 55mph and, under give and take conditions, fuel consumption in the region of 90mpg could be expected. Initially, it was imported into the UK by Bob Foster of Parkstone, Poole, Dorset. If anyone should have known anything about handling it was Bob, a 'works' rider for Moto Guzzi.

Of the early British scooter manufacturers, few machines managed even moderate success. Designed and manufactured by newcomers, production problems eliminated most before they could establish a firm foothold in the

The Swallow Gadabout was Britain's answer to the Vespa and Lambretta but its lack of styling and sophistication meant it never offered either a serious challenge. (Courtesy R. Cordon Champ)

The 192cc Moto Guzzi Galletto, considered by many one of the best scooters made, had large diameter interchangeable wheels and provision for carrying a front-mounted spare. It was virtually a motorcycle enclosed within a metal shell.

marketplace. Others, like the 98cc and 122cc BAC Gazelles, for example, made by the Bond Aircraft and Engineering Company (Blackpool) Ltd. of Long Ridge, Lancashire, seemed to lack even a pretence of styling. They had no rear suspension, either, under the (mistaken) impression that 4.00 x 8 inch balloon tyres would be a substitute. As Swallow soon found out with its Gadabout, a new design had to make visual impact and have a certain degree of sophistication if it was to be considered favourably alongside its Italian-made counterparts.

Projects and Developments Ltd. of Blackburn, and C.B. Harper Aircraft Ltd. of Exeter Airport, were both keen to use fibreglass for the bodywork of their designs, as it has good structural strength, is light in weight, does not corrode and can be shaped easily without need for expensive press tools. Furthermore, it is less inclined to amplify mechanical noise than its metal counterpart and is easy to repair in the event of an accident. Of the two designs, the Oscar, made by Projects and Developments Ltd., made its public debut first at the 1953 Frankfurt Show. A British viewing followed soon afterwards at that year's Earls Court Motor Cycle Show.

The fibreglass bodywork was attached to a duplex tube 'open' frame, fitted with a leading link front fork and pivoting fork rear suspension, both forks being malleable castings. Flexitor bonded rubber units formed the suspension medium, with a single pre-load adjustment. Depending on the purchaser's requirement, either a 122cc or a 197cc fan-cooled single cylinder two-stroke Villiers engine could be specified, with a bolt-up three-speed gearbox. Rubber-mounted in the frame, the power unit had chain final drive. As an optional extra, a Siba electric starter/ignition unit was listed, as was a spare wheel which was interchangeable with either of the two 12 inch diameter steel disc wheels. Moulded in two sections, the rearmost part of the fibreglass bodywork could be raised like a car bonnet to provide access to the engine and transmission. Both models weighed 220lbs. The 122cc Oscar cost £149.8s. and the 197cc version £159.

The Harper Scootamobile was launched a year later. Its bodywork was moulded in Rhiteglass, a glass reinforced plastics material developed by the scooter's designer, Spike Rhiando. It, too, was moulded in two sections, the front one almost completely enveloping the front wheel and housing twin headlamps, separated by a vertical divider. In this design, the rider and passenger sat within, rather than on, the bodywork. This arrangement, on account of its bulbous nature, meant the bodywork had to be recessed at its centre before it broadened out again at the rear, a layout not conducive to an attractive appearance.

The Harper's suspension arrangements were unusual in that the sliders of the telescopic front fork worked inside the stanchions whilst, at the rear, the tube that bridged the pivoting rear fork contained a torsion bar. It permitted up to 7.5 inches of rear wheel movement. Motive power was provided by the ubiquitous 197cc fan-cooled single cylinder Villiers engine with chain final drive via a three-speed gearbox. Both wheels were of 12 inch diameter and interchangeable, and included in the overall specification was a Siba starter. The use of a sturdier and more complex frame than that used in the Oscar accounted for the much heavier weight of 330lbs. Inclusive of Purchase Tax, the Scootamobile was priced at £175.8s. One can only speculate as to why neither the Oscar or the Scootamobile went into production.

The first British manufacturer to make any real impact on the home market was the Dayton Cycle Co. Ltd. of Park Royal, London NW10. Well established as a reputable sports bicycle manufacturer, the company also had the benefit of production and marketing experience. Although its 224cc Albatross scooter lacked the flair of Italian styling, it possessed a certain charm all its own, being seemingly well-built and finished in an attractive, two-tone colour scheme. Part of its success was due to a favourable power to weight ratio, the combination of a 224cc single cylinder Villiers engine with four-speed gearbox, and an overall weight of 280lbs, giving it the edge in terms of performance over many of its contemporaries.

A big machine by scooter standards, the Albatross had an Earles-type front fork and pivoted fork rear suspension controlled by two hydraulically-damped suspension units. The 12 inch diameter pressed steel wheels had split rims and were fitted with lined alloy hubs that contained the 6 inch diameter brake drums. Made in 14 gauge steel, the well-finished bodywork did not envelope the front wheel which, like the Lambretta, had its own separate mudguard that turned over and with the wheel. The Albatross did not have a conventional low floorpan behind the front apron either. In its place a central tunnel had been formed to direct cooling air to the engine, and there were also louvres cut into the panels on either side of the engine to assist with this function. The panels were removable to allow access to the engine and rear wheel.

At the rear, the bodywork could be raised to aid removal of the rear wheel in the event of a puncture. Long footboards ran either side of the bodywork. Rear brake and rocking gearchange pedals slotted through the footboards, the engine being started by a kickstarter alongside the right-hand rear panel. Retailing at £182.14s., the success of the Albatross was underlined by the fact that it remained in production until 1960 - by which time the scooter craze was in decline. It was, perhaps, the only British scooter to be a commercial success.

In the years that followed, the Albatross benefited from a number of improvements. The most significant was the introduction in 1957 of the Albatross Twin, based on the newly introduced and more powerful 249cc Villiers 2T engine unit. The single cylinder model continued alongside it, re-named the Albatross Single; its original 1H unit replaced by the later 246cc 2H Villiers engine. A Siba self-starter had become part of the standard specification.

Dayton also produced a smaller capacity model, the Flamenco, based on a 147cc two-stroke fan-cooled single cylinder Villiers 2L engine. This later design brought in additional income as the bodywork was subsequently sold to Panther and Sun for use on that company's scooters.

The first other than Italian-made scooter to be imported from the Continent was the French-made Motobecane, marketed in 1954 by Motor Imports Co. of London SW9. Described as a utility scooter, the location of its engine and transmission followed Italian practice by being combined as one unit that pivoted at the rear end of the frame. The front fork was of the undamped leading link type, its movement controlled by rubber bands. The rear suspension followed suit, using only a single band.

Production costs were kept down by dispensing with any real enclosure; the frame was of the 'U' type, formed from a single, large diameter steel tube to which legshields and footboards had been added. Known initially as the Scooter AB (later as the Moby Scooter), it had interchangeable 10 inch diameter wheels with a rear-mounted spare and weighed only 165lbs. Stylish in its own way, its main advantage lay in a low retail price of £124.16s. No doubt

To climb BEN NEVIS **Lambretta** chose

CASTROL

TWO-STROKE SELF-MIXING OIL

On Sunday, June 16th, Mr. Geoffrey Parker, a Lambretta representative, climbed Ben Nevis on a standard Model 'D' Lambretta. For this 5-hour gruelling climb in 85 degrees of heat, Lambretta chose Castrol Two-Stroke Self-Mixing Oil.

Follow the experts —
always ask for Castrol by name

All manner of stunts were performed to help sell scooters by demonstrating their reliability and durability. A Lambretta representative climbed Ben Nevis on a standard Model D in the summer of 1957, taking five hours in a temperature of 85 degrees F. (Courtesy Castrol (UK) Ltd.

the importers sold quite a number under the 'easy terms' for which they were renowned as part of the Pride and Clarke organisation.

1955 represented a watershed in the burgeoning scooter market when a host of new models became available. Yet surprisingly, with the sole exception of Douglas, none of the other major British motorcycle manufacturers had yet shown any interest in adding a scooter to their ranges, either of their own design or imported or built under licence. It must have been obvious by now that the scooter was more than just a passing fad.

Scooter riders had their own clubs and magazines and every encouragement to take part in a variety of events ranging from rallies and gymkhanas to those of a more competitive nature. The clubs, some with over 1000 members, ran events catering for scooter riders only, helping to develop a sense of 'togetherness'. Well-known personalities - and many senior public figures - were keen to be seen riding a scooter, the implication being that it was wise and trendy to ride a scooter with its built-in weather protection, freedom from self-mainte-nance and no need for mechanical know-how. Above all else, a scooter exuded a sense of freedom with respectability at a time when running even a cheap, second-hand car was beyond the means of most weekly wage owners, especially the young.

BSA was the first British manufacturer to concede that the scooter market could no longer be overlooked. At the 1955 Motor Cycle Show it presented two of its own designs: the 198cc Beezer and the 70cc Dandy. Although different in concept, both were quite revolutionary in approach; the Beeza breaking new ground by using a single cylinder sidevalve engine and a car-type self-starter.

Both had an unusual engine layout. The Beeza had a forward-facing combined engine and transmission unit, of BSA's own design and manufacture. It was located horizontally, with its light alloy cylinder head and barrel at a right-angle to the main casting, rather like a horizontally-opposed twin that had lost its nearside cylinder. Of the alpha high angle valve type, and having a squish cylinder head, the sidevalve engine was built in unit with a four-speed gearbox, driven via a car-type single plate clutch. Following car practice, a toothed ring around the periphery of the clutch was engaged by the starter motor - a considerable improvement over the Siba electrical arrangement used on other scooters.

With bore and stroke dimensions of 66 x 58mm, the 'oversquare' engine's valves were actuated by rockers rather than cam followers in order to reduce both noise and cost. The main crankcase casting extended rearwards, behind the gearbox, to fully enclose a shaft drive that drove the rear wheel stub axle by bevel gears. The completely assembly pivoted to act as an integral rear swinging arm, its movement controlled by a hydraulically-damped single spring. Also hydraulically damped was the front fork, of the leading link type.

Of pleasing appearance, the metal bodywork comprised a series of pressings attached to light gauge tubing, some of which were quickly detachable to allow access to the engine/transmission assembly. This, and the extensive use of light alloy in the construction of the engine/gear unit, kept the Beeza's overall weight down to 270lbs. An all-in price of £204.12s was quoted at the show, but anyone who placed an order would have been disappointed: the Beeza never went into production after allegedly found lacking in performance.

The 70cc Dandy was an altogether different design, best described as a cross between a step-thru moped and a scooter. Based on a single cylinder overhung crankshaft two-stroke engine of BSA's own design and manufacture, it had a two-speed pre-selector gearbox built in unit, operated by a handlebar control. Where the Dandy broke with convention was the manner in which the engine/gear unit was mounted - horizontally, with the engine on the offside of the rear wheel, its cylinder facing rearward. The gearbox was on its right, the centre section that joined them housing the clutch and an a.c. generator.

Unusual for a British design, the cylinder had a hard, chrome-plated bore in place of a liner, its inlet port above the exhaust port, the flat top piston acting on the Schnurle principle. It was started by a kickstarter which could be hand-operated. The entire engine unit pivoted to provide the rear suspension, a pair of undamped coil springs controlling movement. Final drive was by a fully-enclosed chain. The frame was of the pressed steel 'spine' type, another departure from traditional BSA practice. The fuel tank was below the seat and the front apron had a pair of built-in legshields. Front suspension was of the leading link type, controlled by a helically-wound spring. Both wheels were of 20 inch diameter.

The Dandy was priced at £74.4s., a price maintained when production commenced almost a year after its launch. Teething problems accounted for the delay and continued to afflict it, exacerbated by the inaccessibility of the contact breaker points, a major handicap when carrying out routine maintenance, until production ceased in the early 1960s.

The new generation of scooters had already gone far beyond their maker's original expectations and were in regular use for even serious, long-distance travel. Spike Rhiando had demonstrated these possibilities when, in late 1953, he set off to break the London to Cape record, using a 197cc experimental scooter of his own design. It involved a 10,000 mile journey that included crossing the Sahara Desert. Sadly, the attempt failed, when he had to abort all further progress due to unprecedented cold weather in North Africa. A heavy fall of snow in the Atlas mountains forced him to cover 820 miles in bottom gear, which caused the cooling system to break down. He had, however, successfully crossed the Sahara and covered some 2500 miles. His experience

The BSA Beeza broke new ground and looked as though it would have potential at its 1955 Motor Cycle Show debut. For undisclosed reasons, however, it never went into production and was not seen again.

The BSA Dandy, launched the same time as the Beeza, was just as innovative although It had its faults (not least of which was the inaccessability of the contact breaker) and these persisted until it was dropped from production in the early 60s.

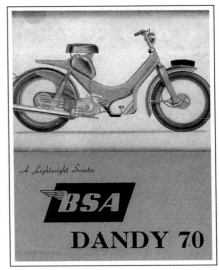

Motorcycling in the 50s

Scooter rallies soon became commonplace. Here, riders from the Vespa Club of West Middlesex are seen gathering outside the Albert Hall in London. (Courtesy Allan Robinson)

was not wasted as it was put to practical use when he launched his Scootamobile a year later.

Maico, the German motorcycle and scooter manufacturer, entered the UK market in 1956, leaving no doubt about the quality of its scooters. The 248cc Maicoletta had a maximum speed of 70mph, whilst the 197cc Mobile was of such vast proportions it was unkindly nicknamed the 'Flying Dustbin'. They were somewhat expensive, at £235.12s and £198 respectively, but even to-day attract attention at classic motorcycle shows, such is their impact. Maico had its own concessionaire in the UK - Maico (Great Britain) Ltd. of London SW7. It also acted as an early importer for Honda when that company entered the UK motorcycle market.

Events of various kinds were now taking scooter riders further and further afield. In 1957, the Vespa Club of Great Britain held its first Isle of Man Scooter Rally. Esso went one better that year by sponsoring the first of several Scoot to Scotland Runs, organised by the Motor Cycling Club. This replaced the Club's hallowed London to Edinburgh Trial, first run in 1904. Initially, the change was not greeted with enthusiasm by the club's more staid members, but it became very popular, with several starting points converging on the road to Scotland at Whitsun.

Eyebrows were raised - in view of the earlier debacle with the ill-fated

Beeza - when BSA re-entered the scooter market in 1958. The new range, marketed under the acquired Sunbeam marque name, comprised three models. The B1 was powered by a single cylinder 173cc two-stroke engine and the B2 and B2S models by a 249cc ohv twin cylinder engine. The 'S' version had an electric starter and 12 volt electrics. Triumph, also in the BSA Group, marketed an identical range of scooters under its own name, the TS1, TW2 and TW2S, which subsequently bore the Tigress name.

The design was based on an open frame, similar to that of the BSA Dandy, which had a single, large diameter, shaped main tube. The engine/gear unit was mounted under the seat and fully enclosed, fan blades attached to the engine's external flywheel keeping it cool. The single cylinder engine was built along conventional lines, but the twin cylinder engine followed car practice, having gear primary transmission and an engine-speed clutch. It was mounted transversely across the frame. All models featured a four-speed gearbox, with

When the BSA Group re-entered the scooter market, it used the Sunbeam name for the BSA version, the alternative being a Triumph Tigress. The model ranges were virtually identical but the Sunbeam versions were dropped when Lady Docker took exception to the colour scheme. (Courtesy Allan Robinson)

The well-engineered Velocette Viceroy scooter arrived on the scene just too late. The first Velocette two-stroke with a petroil lubrication system, it also had a 248cc flat twin engine with reed valves, that later saw service in small hovercraft.

Motorcycling in the 50s

Ironically, the LE Velocette probably came nearest to the industry's long-sought design aimed to attract the person who would never consider purchasing a conventional motorcycle. It lacked the styling of the scooter, however, even though it could be ridden in normal outdoor clothing, as Velocette's sales director, George Denley, demonstrates in Birmingham's traffic.

final drive by chain enclosed within the alloy casting that also acted as the single-sided swinging arm of the rear suspension assembly. The front fork was single-sided, too. Of 10 inch diameter and shod with 3.50 inch section tyres, both wheels ran on stub axles and were quickly detachable.

The 173cc models retailed at £164.19s.8d. and the 249cc twins at £187.2s.6d., or £200.17s for the 12 volt electric start models. All, irrespective of marque, were assembled at BSA's Waverley Street Works in Birmingham. Production continued well into the next decade.

Scooter sales peaked in 1959 at well over 330,000 units sold. It was now too late for any newcomer to jump on the bandwagon, although this did not deter James and Velocette from entering the market in 1960. Even Panther had dropped the Terrot scooter it was importing from France to make its own. As ever, the British motorcycle industry had been too cautious and too slow. When eventually it decided to take the plunge, the scooter market was at the point of decline.

It is fortuitous that the scooter coincided with the pan-European postwar demand for cheap, reliable motorised transport, at a time when buying and running even a small, second-hand car was beyond the means of many. The appearance of the bubble car suggested some form of compromise, where two could travel in relative comfort and with full weather protection. But this could be accomplished only at a leisurely pace and in a vehicle which usually had little pretence of styling or the chic appeal of the scooter. Those who sought really basic motorised transport as a means of commuting found solace firstly in one of the small capacity cyclemotors, which they could add to their bicycle, to take the effort out of pedalling. Later, they graduated to the more sophisticated and fully-fledged moped. Minimum expenditure and very low running costs were the main objectives. The scooter attracted a new class of user, where leisure use was often the decisive factor.

Collectively, all of these new categories of vehicle were responsible for a marked upturn in two-wheeled sales which had increased from 135,045 in 1950 to 331,806 in 1959, and there was a corresponding increase in the number of these vehicles in use from 761,500 in 1950 to a staggering 1,764,535 in 1959. These figures, however, do include three-wheel vehicles such as side-car outfits and bubble cars.

One interesting fact remains. Although reluctant to acknowledge it, the scooter achieved the breakthrough the traditional motorcycle industry had been seeking for so long. It had attracted the type of person who would never have bought a motorcycle, yet longed for a clean, quiet and convenient means of transportation that demanded neither physical effort or protective clothing. The industry must have lost millions promoting causes that only just fell short of the mark. Was it just luck that the scooter filled this gap after it had failed to attract any interest some 40 or so years earlier, or was it because the young found it so trendy? It did, after all, fit in well with the 'pop' scene that was all the rage at that time and did not antagonise parents, to whom a scooter seemed safe and a motorcycle dangerous!

The two-stroke bares its teeth

Little could be done to boost the performance of the average 125cc two-stroke initially, apart from shedding all surplus weight. This is a typical example of how a 125cc two-stroke was prepared for grasstrack racing at Leatherhead in 1950.

Until the fifties, and with a few notable exceptions like the Scott and DKW, the two-stroke motorcycle was expected to serve only a very mundane purpose. Powered by what was little more than a lawnmower engine, it was intended to provide the newcomer with a low-powered introduction to motorcycling, or to act as a reliable and economical form of transport to and from work. Over the years it performed either, and sometimes both, of these roles so well that it became an object of affection. No-one took it seriously when, soon after the war, a 125cc class was introduced to encourage the use of two-strokes in competition. Already eligible to take part in an up to 250cc class, they were usually more than overshadowed by their four-stroke counterparts, so few bothered to enter them.

In competition events, two-strokes were ridden in more or less standard trim, shorn of all surplus parts no longer required to fulfil legal road-going requirements; that is, unless they were to be ridden in a trial where it was necessary to ride on public roads between sections. If high speed events were contemplated, no special parts were available with which to boost engine performance. Tuning had to be limited to polishing the ports or, if the tuner was sufficiently skilled, to enlarge and/or re-profile them, and pad out the crankcase to increase compression. Even then, it was a gamble: few machines then available were capable of sustaining the additional stresses resulting from these modifications.

An insight into how intensive development could make a racing two-stroke competitive against the four-strokes had already presented itself. Ewald Kluge had won the 1938 Lightweight TT on a 250cc DKW twin, fitted with an additional pumping cylinder that acted as a supercharger. He won by more than ten minutes and had broken the lap record by raising it by almost 3mph. In the following year's Junior TT race, Heiner Fleischmann finished third on another DKW, with Kluge taking second place in the Lightweight race. It was said that the DKWs were so noisy they could be heard in Liverpool! What it cost to make these machines so competitive is not known, but it must have been considerable as the Third Reich were striving for success with cost only a secondary consideration.

World War 2 prevented further development continuing along similar lines and, afterward, the FIM (the Federation Internationale Motorcyclist, the body that controls international motorcycle sport) banned the use of superchargers, which had played a significant role in DKW's successes. Furthermore, with the division of Germany into east and west, the DKW factory at Zschopau, in Sachsen, was now in the eastern sector and part of the Communist Bloc. A new company, V.E.B. Motorradwerke (MZ), was set up to take over where DKW had left off. This new company was destined to have the most remarkable influence on the development of high performance two-strokes in later years.

Much to Britain's shame, two-stroke development was left mainly to the Continental manufacturers, so that the British-made two-stroke plodded on much as before. Initially, British manufacturers were content to leave it to a few enthusiastic amateurs to show how the two-stroke could be adapted, with relatively little effort or expense, to meet the four-strokes on more equal terms. Foremost amongst these had been Tommy Meeten, who made it his life's cause to make British two-strokes more competitive. Sadly, he met with little success.

Times were changing, however. Looking firstly at trials, by the beginning of 1950, BSA and James were already offering trials models, two of them from the latter company based on factory machines ridden in 'open' trials and the ISDT the previous year. Other manufacturers soon followed, as most trials now included a class for small capacity two-strokes.

It may be thought that riding a two-stroke of small capacity with trials gearing amounted to a self-imposed handicap, especially as trade-supported trials called for a considerable amount of road work between sections. The Colmore, for example, followed a 74 mile route, and the Victory one of 60 miles. Yet it was no deterrent to the devoted, as demonstrated when Mike Riley won the Moxon Cup in the Best Under 150cc Class in the 1950 Colmore, riding a 122cc DMW. Perhaps inappropriately, Johnny Brittain won the Francis Barnett Cup for the Best Under 150cc Class in that year's Victory - riding a 122cc James! A few, like Sid Goddard, were really determined to demonstrate the versatility of a two-stroke: he entered the 1950 Exeter Trial with a lightweight single seat sidecar attached to his 197cc Ambassador. It was a brave attempt but he was unable to claim an award.

The premier trial of the year, the Scottish Six Days, had included an up to 200cc Class since the war, and from 1948 on had a 125cc Class, won by Mike Riley in 1950 on a 122cc DMW. It was Ralph Venables, however, who had the initiative to organise, on behalf of the Sunbeam MCC, a two-stroke trial with 15 observed sections that November. Run over a 17 mile course at Liphook,

The ubiquitous 123cc BSA Bantam represented an early attempt to sell an over-the-counter competition model, produced specifically for use in trials. The rider is Bill Polley, a well-known clubman in the Brighton area.

Motorcycling in the 50s

The 197cc Villiers-engined James Colonel was a very successful early trials model, especially in the hands of Bill Lomas. He won the 1951 Travers Trophy Trial - regarded as the most arduous trial to be held for many years - on one of these models.

in Hampshire, it attracted an entry of 12 and was won by Bill Thorne on a 197cc James. The Newcomer's Award went to another James rider, a young Triss Sharp riding in his first competition event.

The first major breakthrough was made during April 1951, when Bill Lomas surprised everyone by winning the Travers Trophy Trial with a loss of only 9 marks, four of them on time. Pitted against an entry of 112, his mount was a 197cc James. The going was difficult, as snow had fallen the night before and he had to contend with both ice and snow. It was no one-off success either, as towards the end of the year he won the Northern Experts Trial on the same machine and in totally different conditions, with the loss of only 17 marks. Two-stroke trials models began to get very popular!

A news item during May 1951 that could easily have been overlooked related to Invacar, a company that made two-stroke powered invalid carriages in Thundersley, Essex. Invacar had made two prototype competition two-strokes using an ingenious rubber in torsion suspension system, to be marketed under the Greeves name, the surname of Invacar's founder, Bert Greeves. Nothing more was heard for several years but, as will soon become evident, this small company contributed significantly to the two-stroke's advancement in motorcycle sport during the years that lay ahead.

Francis Barnett, like several of the other lightweight two-stroke manufacturers, displayed a Villiers-engined 197cc Falcon 60 competition model at the 1951 Motor Cycle Show. This company had been providing works-supported entries before this and had enjoyed a reasonable amount of success in trade-supported trials. It was on one of its 197cc models that the most significant step forward yet took place, when Jack Botting put up the best class performance in the 1950 British Experts Trial. Jack had offset the engine in the frame to give clearance for a 4 inch section rear tyre to be fitted, which made his machine more competitive. Others soon followed suit. On a 122cc model, Brian Martin won the 150cc award in the 1951 Victory, Kickham and Mitchell Trials. It did not escape attention, either, that in the 1951 Southern Experts Trial Brian had made the only clean climb of Empshott Stairs, which had defeated every four-stroke entered.

Early in 1952, details were released of a prototype 197cc James. This broadly followed the specification of the Francis Barnett, but used instead a 7E Villiers engine, the tuned version of the 6E. It had a lugless frame with the tube ends butt welded.

Sun introduced its 197cc Challenger trials model at the end of March. It had taken the bold step of adding plunger-type rear suspension at a time when most trials riders were positively convinced that a rigid frame was essential for success. Opinions were beginning to waver, however, after Fred Barnes rode an Excelsior Talisman Twin fitted with pivoted fork rear suspension in the 1952 Scottish Six Days Trial. He finished, to claim a Second Class Award.

When DMW announced its new model range for 1953, the competition models had plunger-type rear suspension, as did the models from Dot, although the latter could also offer the option of pivoted fork rear suspension, if required.

Francis Barnett seemed to be making the most progress in 1952 when Arthur Shutt won the Lomax Trial, A.H.L. Humphries the South Downs Trial and Ernie Whiffen the Traders' Trophy Trial. But before the trials riding season drew to an end, Bill Lomas took a brilliant fourth place on a 197cc James in the British Experts Trial, run in blizzard-like conditions in the Cotswolds. Bill's moustache had icicles in it at the finish!

Norman Cycles Ltd. of Ashford, Kent showed a Villiers-engined 197cc rigid frame competition model at the 1952 Motor Cycle Show, with the option of a 122cc engine. Road racer Arthur Wheeler had ridden the 197cc version in that year's 'Wayzegoose' Press Trial. It was built along similar lines to the Francis Barnett models. Only a short while afterwards, James disclosed it would be selling a replica of its 'works' model, the 197cc Commando, that had been ridden with such success by Bill Lomas. Not only would it be fitted with the better 7E Villiers engine but, if required, could be supplied with a new four-speed gearbox. Handling on the rough had been improved by fitting a two-way hydraulically damped telescopic front fork and a 4 inch section rear tyre.

That Francis Barnett retained the upper hand in trials throughout 1953 was highlighted when George Fisher won the Kickham Trial on a 197cc model, without losing a single mark. A.M.L. McLean, similarly mounted, won the Scottish Experts, losing only 4 marks. The biggest surprise came in the Northern Experts Trial, when Arthur Shutt and Eric Adcock, each on a 197cc model, tied with T.E. Leach's 490cc Norton. Leach emerged the eventual victor, but only after winning the brake test that acted as a decider.

Dot decided to put all its eggs in one basket at the end of the 1953 season and market only competition models. For 1954 three 197cc trials models and three 197cc scramblers were offered. The power unit in each case was the new 8E Villiers, available with a three or four-speed gearbox. For an extra payment of £3.10s (£3.50) the trials model engine could be 'works' tuned; if the optional four-speed gearbox was specified, that added a further £6. There was also the hint of a new trials model powered by a 2T Villiers twin cylinder engine.

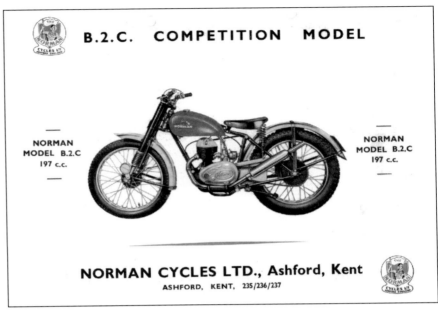

B.2.C. COMPETITION MODEL

NORMAN MODEL B.2.C 197 c.c.

NORMAN MODEL B.2.C 197 c.c.

NORMAN CYCLES LTD., Ashford, Kent

ASHFORD, KENT, 235/236/237

The Norman B2C trials model was a thoroughly workman-like job, powered by Villiers' 197cc 7E competition engine. The contribution made by this Ashford, Kent-based factory is all too easily overlooked.

Motorcycling in the 50s

DMW's plans for 1954 went awry when problems arose over the supply of Villiers engines. A tentative arrangement was made with a French engine manufacturer, Ateliers de Mechanique du Centre, in an attempt to overcome this hitch. However, whatever the problem had been with Villiers it was soon resolved, and Villiers engines continued to be fitted into the new square section tube frame, which had a pressed steel centre section and pivoted fork rear suspension. A prototype of this frame, fitted with a 7E Villiers engine, was ridden by Mollie Briggs in the 1953 ISDT.

Although the rider of a lightweight two-stroke could now compete on better terms in trials with a four-stroke rider, progress was still slow. However, it should be remembered that the majority of results listed all related to the 'open' trade-supported type of event, in which an up-and-coming two-stroke rider had to compete against the acknowledged four-stroke experts. It was in the lesser events organised at regional or club level that the trials two-stroke was really beginning to score.

A good example of this is the 1954 Three Musketeers Trial, organised by the South Reading MCC. Upgraded to a regional restricted event that year, it attracted 171 entries, 20 of them sidecars, and was run over a 20 mile course that contained a dozen observed sections. It started and finished at California-in-England, near Wokingham. Peter Stirling on a 197cc James, an up-and-coming two-stroke rider, won the Three Musketeers Trial, losing 31 marks, whilst Geoff Robertson, on a 122cc Francis Barnett, lost 69 marks to put up the Best Performance up to 175cc. Ray Peacock took the Best 250cc award with his 197cc Norman (35 marks lost). Interestingly, Peter Stirland finished just one mark ahead of the Best 350cc rider, Gordon Jackson on a four stroke 'works' AJS! The Best South Reading Club Member was John Richards (197cc James), and Cliff Washington, on a similar machine, was the Best Southern Centre Member with a loss of 41 marks. *Motor Cycling's* reporter needed little confirmation that this had been a two-stroke day, especially when, on a difficult sub-section, all but two of the 19 'clean' solo climbs had been made by riders of Villiers-powered lightweights.

The 197cc Dot TDH-X trials model enjoyed a fair measure of success in the early 1950s, although nothing like that of the company's scrambles model. Options were available for three- or four-speed gearboxes and a 'works' tuned trials engine could also be fitted for a moderate extra sum at the time of ordering.

A minor setback in the 200cc class occurred when Triumph introduced its 149cc Terrier four-stroke. An example was obtained and converted by Jim Alves so that he could ride it in trials. He and the Terrier made their first 'open' debut in the 1954 Colmore Cup Trial, in which he lost only 6 marks, to put up the Best Solo Performance and win the Colmore Cup. Even so, it was Peter Stirland who won the Calthorpe Cup for the Best up to 250cc performance on his 197cc James (22 marks lost) and Ernie Smith (122cc Francis Barnett) the Moxon Cup, after losing 20 marks, to claim the Best up to 150cc award. The event still favoured a lengthy course - 69 miles this year - and attracted 127 solos and 21 sidecars.

Dot — DEVON de TROVE

Thoroughbreds for Scrambles,

Model TDH-X

Trials honours were shared between James and Francis Barnett in 1954. The most outstanding achievement was when George Fisher was runner-up in the Scottish Six Days Trial on his 122cc Francis Barnett, with the loss of only 67 marks. His reward for this remarkable effort was the Lochaber Challenge Trophy, for it was not until the fifth day that he had to concede victory to Artie Ratcliffe on a 350cc 'works' Matchless. Artie won with only two marks less.

Sammy Miller made his debut in that year's Scottish Six Days Trial, riding his home-built SHS. He put up such a good performance that he won the Ben Nevis Challenge Trophy, awarded for the second-best performance by a Scottish Trial newcomer who had not won a name trophy or class award in a trade-supported trial. Sammy had ridden his SHS to Belfast Docks to embark for Glasgow where, on arrival, he wheeled off the boat and rode it to Edinburgh, his few possessions carried in a haversack strapped to the petrol tank. His homeward journey was made the same way - often the only way an unsupported amateur rider could get to and from events in those days. James regained the competitive edge throughout the 1955 season, aided early on by Sammy Miller who won the 250cc award in the Hurst Cup Trial riding one of their 197cc models. John Houghton on another won the Cotswold Cups Trial, beating experts such as Jim Alves, Bob Ray and Peter Stirland, the last-mentioned now riding for Royal Enfield. Houghton continued his run of successes by winning the Clayton Trial and then the Mitchell Trial, losing only three marks in each of these three trials. Able support from Jack Simpson and Bryan Povey gave James the Team Award in the Mitchell.

George Fisher kept Francis Barnett's hopes alive by again winning the Lochaber Challenge Trophy in the Scottish Six Days Trial. Riding a 201cc model, only one mark separated him from the winner, Jeff Smith. Sadly, this proved to be Fisher's last major success whilst riding for Francis Barnett. At the end of the season he signed with Triumph to ride instead a 199cc Tiger Cub four stroke. His defection was mourned by trials two-stroke enthusiasts, although their hopes were not dashed entirely. Bill Jackson won the Manville Cup Trial on a 197cc Francis Barnett, and Arthur Shutt, also on a 197cc model, the Northern Experts Trial.

Although the James Commando had proved the most successful trial two-stroke in 1955, underlined by Bill Martin's win in that year's John Douglas Trial, it may be wondered why Bill Lomas no longer figured more prominently. The answer was simple; he could ride for James only when his professional and international road racing commitments permitted.

The two-stroke trials enjoyed fewer successes throughout the 1956 season, even though both James and Francis Barnett featured pivoted fork rear suspension, two years after it had appeared on the scrambles models. Soon, James and Francis Barnett would be handicapped by the dictates of their parent company, Associated Motor Cycles Limited, which would compel them to forsake the Villiers engine in favour of the new Piatti-designed two-stroke engine of their own manufacture. The competition models had a brief reprieve before this was implemented as problems with the standard road-going production models fitted with this engine had first to be eliminated. When it was fitted eventually to the competition models, it brought to light additional problems, not the least of which was its greater width and different power characteristics. James and Francis Barnett had a heavy commercial burden to bear from then on.

Dot showed up a little better in trials that year when Eric Adcock won the

Francis Barnett's competition models suffered a self-imposed handicap when the bought-in Villiers engine was replaced by the company's own Piatti-designed equivalent. Initially unreliable, this problem was overcome, but the engine was a much wider unit to accommodate than its predecessor and had different power characteristics. The Trials 83 model had been developed from the Scrambler 82 design, also AMC-engined.

Bill Martin was no mean performer with the 249cc AMC-engined James. Here he is concentrating hard in the March 1959 Kickham Trial. He has since managed to regain possession of one of the factory models he once rode. (Courtesy B.R. Nicholls)

Lomax Trial and Doug Chadwick the Manx Two-Day Trial, followed by the Manville Cup Trial. The best result came from Phil Beal, though, who won the Ben Nevis Trophy in the Scottish Six Days Trial. All were riding a 197cc Villiers-engined model.

E. Greenup won the Valente Trial on a 197cc model to keep Francis Barnett in the hunt, and was runner-up in the Lion Two-Day Trial. John Houghton made sure James was in the running, too, by winning the Best Two-Stroke Award in the Red Rose Trial. Bryan Povey added his weight by winning the Reliance Trial on an over-bored 201cc model. DMW made a welcome re-appearance when A.M.L. McLean claimed the Alan Hay Memorial Award in the Scottish Six Days Trial, riding a 197cc model. A pointer to the future lay in the results of this year's famous trial. The Edinburgh Trophy had been awarded to J. Pudil on a 150cc CZ for the Best Performance by a non-British subject.

All motorcycle sporting events ground to a halt in mid-December, when the deepening Suez crisis re-introduced the need for fuel rationing. A couple of months passed before the government could be persuaded to make a petrol allowance available for a limited number of trade-supported events, even though motorcycles were still an important export earner and competition successes helped sell them.

The Bemrose was the first 'petrol-privileged' trial to be run in 1957, of necessity over a shortened 35 mile route. Jon Tye won the 250cc class on a 147cc Francis Barnett. In the earlier Alan Trophy Trial., E. Greenup won the 250cc award on a 197cc Francis Barnett, 11 marks ahead of Gordon McLaughlan's 350cc AJS, whilst in the Traders Cup Trial A Jones won the appropriately-named Tiddlers Trophy on a 147cc Francis

Barnett. When petrol rationing ended in time for June's Cambrian Trial, Jones won the Bert James Cup for the Best up to 175cc Performance on the same machine.

James re-asserted itself when Garth Weldon won the Committee's Cup on a 201cc James in the Bemrose Trial. Ken Holloway, also on a James, won the 200cc Award in the Travers Trophy Trial and Rob Hart the 200cc Award in the Lomax Cup Trial.

With Triumph's 199cc Tiger Cub four-stroke having replaced the earlier 149cc Terrier model, the appearance of 'works' entered Tiger Cub competition models made it more difficult for the trials two-strokes to make headway in 1957. Roy Peplow adapted so well to the Tiger Cub that he won the 250cc class in the Welsh Trophy, Clayton Trophy, Red Rose and Greensmith Trials, capping them all by winning the Mitchell Trial outright. Garth Weldon salvaged something for James by winning the 200cc award in the Mitchell and, switching to a 147cc model, the Boakes and Harper Trophy for the Best 175cc Performance in the Cotswold Cups Trial. James Houghton and his 197cc James denied Peplow the 250cc award in this event and took the 200cc award in the West of England Trial the following weekend, Bryan Povey having won the trial outright on a 201cc James. It gave James the Team Award.

If James and Francis Barnett had lost some ground during the year, Greeves could be partly to blame with Peter Hammond claiming the 200cc award in the Cambrian and Manx Two Days Trials. Jack Simpson won the 250cc award in the Perce Simon and Mitcham Vase Trials, whilst another destined for fame in the years ahead - Dave Bickers - won the 250cc award in the Eastern Experts Trial. All the Greeves riders rode 197cc models.

Arthur Shutt was one of the mainstays of the Francis Barnett competition team in both trials and scrambles, but was more successful in the latter. Here he is riding a 249cc AMC-engined trials model in the November 1958 Southern Trial. (Courtesy B.R. Nicholls)

Dot and Francis Barnett just about managed to stay in the hunt, when Eric Adcock won the 250cc award in the Southern and Hoad Trophies Trials on his 197cc Dot. J.M. Davies won the 250cc award in the Scottish Experts Trial on a 197cc Francis Barnett.

The Triumph Tiger Cub remained dominant throughout the 1958 season, winning six of the year's major trials. James was now relegated to the role of second runner with successes mainly in the lower capacity classes. John Houghton won the Clayton Trial on a 197cc model, and Bill Martin, on a 201cc model, the West of England Trial. Eric Adcock's overall victory in the Highland Two-Day Trial on a 197cc Dot, followed by two further wins in the Greensmith and Reliance Trials (this time on a 249cc model) helped keep Dot in the running.

Bill Faulkner responded on behalf of Francis Barnett by winning the

Brian Stonebridge, towering above his 250cc Greeves, also rode in trials, though not with anything like the level of success in enjoyed in scrambles. This shot was taken during the 1958 South Midland Team Trial. (Courtesy B.R. Nicholls)

Motorcycling in the 50s

Cambrian Trial. Although the Greeves competition models had already benefited from the attentions of Brian Stonebridge's and no longer used a frame identical to that of the road bikes, their only major success came late in the year when Bryan Povey won the Manville Cup Trial on a 249cc model. He had left James to ride for Greeves.

When the 1959 trials season opened, the two-strokes were up against even keener competition from a new generation of four-strokes. Although the Tiger Cub continued its run of successes as the front runner, an additional threat came from BSA, whose 249cc C15 unit-construction model lent itself to use in trials; as far back as 1957 Brian Martin had been riding a factory prototype trials version as part of the company's development programme. In Brian's hands, the C15T acquitted itself well and after he had won the 1958 Southern Experts Trial, BSA decided to equip its trials team with C15Ts. They got off to a promising start when the St. David's Trial, the first trade-supported trial of the year, was won outright by Jeff Smith. John Draper and Brian Martin, his two teammates, did sufficiently well for BSA to be awarded the Manufacturers' Team Award.

If anything, the 1959 trials season proved a barren year for outright wins by any trials two-stroke. The only exceptions went in favour of James, when J.L. Harris and W. Jackson Jnr won the first and third stages respectively of the Inter-Centre Team Trial at Brecon, and J.H. Roberts the Lomax Trial. However, it should be appreciated that, quite apart from the successes enjoyed by the Triumph and BSA four-strokes, Sammy Miller was setting an unparalleled record of success on his 500cc single cylinder Ariel four-stroke. Even so, nothing could overshadow Roy Peplow's success in the 1959 Scottish Six Days Trial, which he won on a 199cc Tiger Cub, losing only 16 marks. In just three seasons the trials version of the Tiger Cub offered a serious challenge to the trials two-strokes which, until then, were beginning to show their supremacy, even in trade-supported events.

Looking now at scrambles, clubs organising these events were at first reluctant to include a lower capacity class for two-strokes in their programmes. It seemed improbable that these small capacity machines would have enough speed to make such a race entertaining, yet alone prove robust enough to withstand the pounding they were likely to receive. Someone had to bite the bullet and it was the North Hants Club that added a 125cc class in a 1950 scramble. Run over six laps of an eased course, it attracted just four riders, and was won by Eric Cheney on a 122cc OEC. The later Cotswold Scramble included a 125cc class, too, which was won by Bill Nicholson on a factory-prepared BSA Bantam.

Two-stroke successes in scrambles were still few and hardly made the headlines. It was not until Dot announced it would be adding a Villiers-engined 197cc scrambles model to its range that things began to look up. Few could have anticipated the impact that this small, Manchester-based company would have on scrambles during the years that followed

Dot was quick to capitalise on its newly-introduced 197cc scrambler by adding a 122cc 'works' model. At the 1951 Hawkstone Scramble Bill Barugh won the 125cc class convincingly, leading from start to finish. He was to prove the mainstay of the Dot scrambles team for many years to follow, with an enviable record of consistency and outright wins.

OEC, never hesitant to experiment, launched its own competition model at the end of the year, fitted with pivoted fork rear suspension. By adding a

countershaft with a cross-over drive to keep the centre of the final drive sprocket in line with that of the rear fork pivot, the tension of the final drive chain remained constant. No other manufacturer could boast this desirable feature, yet it never caught on. The drawback was the added complication and the need to use three chains, one of which had a very short run and would wear rapidly.

By 1952, Dot showed it was a force to reckon with in scrambles; in that year's Sunbeam MCC Point to Point not only did Bill Barugh, Bryan Sharp and Arthur Vincent take the first three places in the 200cc race, but also the Manufacturers' Team Prize. The same trio, supported by other Dot riders such as Terry Cheshire, E. Webster and W.H. Wood, dominated the 125cc and 200cc classes in most of the major scrambles that year. Cheekily, they even ventured into the 201cc to 350cc class, much to the chagrin of many works four-stroke riders who were accustomed to regarding this class as exclusively their own. They were definitely not amused when Bill Barugh won the 350cc class of the Dartmoor Scramble on a 201cc Dot, with Terry Cheshire backing him up in third place!

Throughout 1953 Dot continued to dominate the lightweight classes in scrambles, with a particularly stout-hearted effort at Shrubland Park, taking not only the first four places in the Ultra Lightweight Race but also the Manufacturers' Team Prize. Then, thanks to the combined efforts of Messrs. Barugh and Cheshire, aided and abetted by Arthur Vincent and Don Howlett, the first two places in the Lightweight Race went to Dot as well.

When, at the end of the 1953 season Dot declared its intention to manufacture only competition models, an extra £5 would ensure the provision of a 'works' tuned 197cc 8E Villiers engine for the SCH scrambles model. An optional four-speed gearbox was also available for this model on payment of a further £6 and, if required, an Earles-type front fork for £5 more.

If anything, Dot was even more dominant in the 1954 scrambles season, thanks largely to Bill Barugh and the Sharp brothers, Triss and Bryan, who were now riding for the Dot factory. Having amassed such a galaxy of talent, Dot was able to run two factory teams and it was the 'A' team, comprising Stu Bickerton, Don Howlett and Triss Sharp, that won the Manufacturers' Team Award at the 1954 Sunbeam Point to Point. There had been little doubt about the outcome after Triss Sharp and Bill Barugh finished first and second respectively in the 200cc race.

More Dot successes followed in the Hants Grand National, the Cumberland Grand National and in the Hawkstone Park, Dartmoor, Cotswold and Shrubland Park scrambles. At the Cumberland scramble, Bill Barugh really pulled out all the stops to finish second in the 350cc event! It was largely due to the efforts of one man - Arthur Shutt - that Francis Barnett were able to offer Dot some serious competition at times.

Trials and Competition Events. **Dot**

Stripped Scrambler Model SCH

Dot's SCH Scrambles model could be supplied with a number of options, like the Trials model, which included an Earles-type front fork and a 'works' tuned engine. Dot scramblers spearheaded the two-stroke's breakthrough in the early 1950s.

Motorcycling in the 50s

A familiar face and helmet, but an unusual mount. Geoff Duke rides a Dot in a 1956 scramble held in his native Isle of Man. (Courtesy B.R. Nicholls)

More at home (and much more successful) in scrambles, Brian Stonebridge is caught in full flight winning the 250cc Race at a 1957 Shrubland Park event. He appears to be wearing ex-WD riding gear that at one time was very commonplace. His relaxed riding style made it look so easy! (Courtesy B.R. Nicholls)

No-one was really surprised when Dot lost the competitive edge during the 1955 season due to mounting challenge from other manufacturers. Triss and Bryan Sharp were now riding for Francis Barnett and Brian Stonebridge had joined BSA after leaving Matchless, which gave him access to the BSA Bantam. 'Works' 123cc Bantams made a brief comeback in the Experts Grand National when the 150cc race was won by Stonebridge, the Taft brothers taking second and third places. Stonebridge also won that year's Shrubland Park 125cc race, with Triss Sharp (Francis Barnett) and Bill Barugh (Dot) snapping at his heels.

The honours for Francis Barnett, now in the ascendancy, were shared between Triss and Bryan Sharp in the 200cc class of the Hants Grand National, Cheshire Moto-Cross, Dartmoor, Isle of Man Grand National and Cotswold Scrambles. These results didn't leave much room for anyone else!

Throughout the 1956 season, Dot and Francis Barnett found themselves almost evenly matched; Dot having recruited the Rickman brothers and John Avery to help boost its competition efforts. The Experts Grand National and the Shrubland Park scrambles were now about the only major events with a separate 125cc class, and both remained the province of the 'works' entered BSA Bantams, with Stonebridge always in the hunt, this year aided by John Draper and Peter Hammond. Triss and Bryan Sharp remained Francis Barnett's front runners, with strong support from Arthur Shutt.

The start of the 1957 season had been handicapped by a shortage of petrol due to the Suez crisis, but when it resumed a new two-stroke scrambles challenger appeared in the shape of Greeves. Brian Stonebridge had joined the team in January after leaving BSA, and set the scene by winning the 250cc race in ABC's Television Scramble on a 197cc model. An insight into what was soon to follow occurred when he finished third in the sponsor's Television Race on the same machine, which was open to allcomers! Riding the same 197cc Greeves, he won the following day's 250cc race at Boltby Bank and was second in the later Northern Moto-Cross Race, pitted against 500cc four-stroke riders such as BSA's Jeff Smith and Ariel's Ron Langston.

This was definitely Greeves' year, with Brian Stonebridge gaining the reputation of a giant killer. In the Lancashire Grand National he won the Lightweight Race, successfully holding off the 197cc Dots ridden by Bill Barugh and Norman Crooks. At the Hawkstone Park Moto-Cross Grand Prix he rode a 248cc Greeves in the 500cc Invitation Race and won his heat. The other heat winner was Ron Langston on his 497cc Ariel four stroke, yet Brian relegated him to second place in the final! He also took the prize for the fastest 250. Two weeks later, riding a 197cc Greeves, he won the 250cc race in the Experts Grand National and finished third on the same machine in the 175cc to 350cc race, chasing Andy Lee and John Avery on their 'works' BSAs.

An almost identical performance followed at the 1957 Shrubland Park Grand National, where Brian's 197cc Greeves was outpaced only by Jeff Smith's 499cc 'works' BSA. Amazingly, the results were repeated yet again at the August Hawkstone Park Scramble. Brian Stonebridge's performance was becoming predictable, no matter how strong the opposition.

Although the Greeves had by now become the most competitive two-stroke in scrambles, Dot held on tenaciously throughout the 1958 season and these two manufacturers virtually dominated the lightweight class. Francis Barnett made the occasional intervention, but even Triss and Bryan Sharp were finding their challenge blunted by the enforced use of AMC's own two-stroke engines. By the end of the season the Sharp brothers forsook their allegiance to the Coventry factory and signed with Greeves. Although most of the AMC competition engine's problems had been successfully overcome, these engines still offered an uneasy compromise when compared with their Villiers counterparts.

Greeves was now encroaching on the Junior class by using overbored 250s, and with a surprising level of success, too. By the end of 1958 the balance had swung even further in its favour, largely because of another up-and-coming rider, Dave Bickers. A small blip on the horizon appeared at this time which was to prove of greater significance much later on. In the 1958 Thirsk Grand National, the 250cc class was won by W. Oesterle, riding a 247cc Maico two-stroke made in West Germany. The Maico was destined to become almost unbeatable in scrambles, to the exclusion of almost everything else.

As mentioned in the review of the

For a while, Dot experimented with the Villiers 2T twin engine in scrambles which the Rickman brothers had a chance to try, as is evident from this photograph taken at a Shrubland Park scramble in 1958. The rider is Don Rickman. (Courtesy B.R. Nicholls)

progress of the two-stroke in trials, when the 199cc Triumph Tiger Cub trials model first appeared it offered an almost immediate threat to the trials two-strokes. A 199cc Tiger Cub scrambles model had also been produced yet, surprisingly, its only major success was when John Stallard won the 200cc class of the 1959 Hawkstone Park Scramble. Its potential in scrambles could be discounted.

The scrambles version of BSA's 247cc C15 BSA four-stroke presented an altogether different prospect. It became available in 1959 and, by mid-season, was already beginning to make its presence felt in the capable hands of 'works' riders such as Jeff Smith, Arthur Lampkin and Brian Martin.

The Greeves remained the most successful scrambles two-stroke throughout 1959, due mainly to the efforts of Brian Stonebridge and Dave Bickers, with support from Mike Jackson and Norman Crooks, amongst others. Dot's strength lay in its new generation of riders, such as Pat Lamper, Alan Clough, Gerry Scarlett and Joe Johnson.

Until the 1958 season there had been little scope for lightweight two-strokes in scrambles of international status, a situation that changed when a 250cc Coup d'Europe Moto-Cross was introduced that year. Initially, it was the foreign two-strokes - such as Maico, Husqvarna and Jawa/CZ - which made most of the running on the Continent. However, in the British round of the new championship a second place by Brian Stonebridge on a Greeves and a third for Triss Sharp on a Francis Barnet showed British two-strokes were in with a chance. For the 1959 Coupe Brian Stonebridge and Dave Bickers mounted an even more serious challenge which resulted in Brian finishing second in that year's Championship.

It looked as though Brian would have stood a real chance of winning the championship in 1960 had not fate intervened. During October 1959, when returning with Bert Greeves from a visit to Bradford, their car was involved in a head-on collision. Although Bert received only minor injuries, Brian was killed. The news stunned the whole of the motorcycling community and meant Greeves suffered a particularly harmful body blow, losing the driving force behind its competition effort. Brian was that rare combination of brilliant rider and very talented development engineer. His death threw a great deal of responsibility onto the shoulders of Dave Bickers, who responded well to the unexpected demand. Fortunately, he had by now been joined by Triss and Bryan Sharp who had left Francis Barnett at the end of 1959 to sign with Greeves. Although other technicians followed in Brian's footsteps, Greeves'

Dave Bickers was Greeves heir apparent in scrambles, and took over after Brian Stonebridge lost his life in a road accident during October 1959. Dave very soon established an equally impressive record of success and soon became a household name due to the frequency of his wins on a Greeves in the televised scrambles. (Courtesy B.R. Nicholls)

competition shop was never quite the same without the six foot-plus giant of a man (in every sense of the word) whose genius put the Thundersley factory on the road to fame.

Having looked at the progress made by the lightweight two-stroke in trials and scrambles, one surprising fact emerges. Contrary to expectation, the two-stroke made most headway and posed more of a threat to its four-stroke counterpart in scrambles. Furthermore, now that an interest was, at last, being shown in two-stroke engine development, it began to make an impact in every branch of motorcycle sport. To complete the picture, one more area remains to be looked at; that of road racing.

From an historical background, the BSA Bantam stood the best chance of development for racing, as it was a mirror image of Germany's prewar DKW RT125 two-stroke. War reparation resulted in the allied occupation forces obtaining the design details and engineering drawings of the RT125 which allowed BSA to manufacture a mirror copy with the kickstart and gearchange levers on the right-hand side. Initially, manufacture (for export) of the engine only was envisaged, but it was subsequently decided to produce a complete machine using cycle parts of BSA's own design and manufacture. When the 123cc D1 model was launched in June 1948, it was soon followed by a competition version, intended for use in trials. The Bantam had arrived.

John Hogan, as good a rider as he was an engine tuner, soon found the Bantam engine would respond surprisingly well to tuning, despite the enforced use of 'pool' petrol and no special 'performance parts' being available. Riding a much modified, road-going Bantam, he invariably won the Ultra-Lightweight class that was now included in short circuit road race meeting programmes. His race average speeds of 56mph at Blandford and 57mph at Thruxton were by no means uncommon.

The Bantam was, of course, nothing like competitive enough to offer a serious challenge to the Italian four-strokes of similar capacity and never would be. Hogan's contribution was, nevertheless, valuable for bringing road racing on the cheap within the realms of amateur enthusiasts. In its basic form a new road-going Bantam cost only £63.3s.6d and what could be made of it was then down to the owner's expertise in engine preparation.

It is worth recounting that as higher rpm and stresses increased well beyond manufacturers' expectations, additional and often unexpected problems were likely to arise. It was by no means unusual for flywheel generators to burst due to increased centrifugal force, especially the Villiers units which were made of brass. The resultant flying debris could cause additional damage to the engine and rider.

Villiers was drawn into road racing when Dot, using the Villiers 122cc 10D engine unit, decided to enter a team in the newly-introduced Ultra-Lightweight race in the 1951 TT. There were 32 entries in this class and it was a Dot, ridden into seventh place by Eric Hardy, that was the first British machine to finish. Although his race average speed was some 17mph down on that of the winner, he, and the other two members of the Dot team (Guy Newman and Chris Horn), put up a sufficiently good performance for Dot to claim the Manufacturers' Team prize.

Dr Josef Ehrlich must have been encouraged by this result as he decided to add a little more colour (and noise!) by commencing production of a 124cc EMC-Puch two-stroke road racer at his Southall, Middlesex, factory.

John Hogan's run of successes with his 123cc road racing BSA Bantam

Motorcycling in the 50s

continued until 1952, although Fred Burman showed the potential of the new 124cc EMC-Puch when he finished second to Hogan in the 125cc race at Motor Cycling's Silverstone Saturday meeting. It may have caused Hogan to rethink his plans because, when entries were submitted for the 1952 Ultra-Lightweight TT, he entered on an EMC-Puch, as did Noel Mavrogordato, another two-stroke fanatic. Of the three EMC-Puch entries, only Burman finished, in sixth place at 63.14mph. His average speed was more than 12mph down on the race-winning speed of Cecil Sandford's single cylinder dohc MV.

Signs of activity were now becoming apparent from behind the Iron Curtain when a new racing two-stroke was produced in the old DKW works at Zschopau, East Germany. It appeared as the IFA125 at the 1952 Leipzig Fair, bearing a close resemblance to the old RT125, Spain, too, showed an interest in racing two-strokes when Alfonso Mila entered a 125cc Montesa in the 1952 German Grand Prix.

Unfortunately, the British road racing two-strokes failed to show much progress in events of national or international status because the Italian four-strokes continued to outpace them by an ever-increasing margin. Undoubtedly, John Hogan and others had paved the way to making road racing a more economic proposition for amateur riders, in many cases starting them on a career that would blossom as they progressed to much faster machinery. But that was about the limit for the time being, even though 'go faster' parts were becoming available, such as the proprietary George Todd cylinder head for the BSA Bantam.

No mention has been made of the 250cc class in road racing simply because Britain had nothing to offer - either two- or four-stroke - that was in any way competitive. Many years would pass before the East German IFA was transformed into the MZ to make the first really significant contribution to two-stroke engine development, largely due to the efforts of MZ's development engineer, Walter Kaaden. Only then did the road racing two-stroke really come into its own.

Looking at the two-stroke scene as a whole, this previously neglected type of engine really began to show its potential - and its teeth - during the fifties. It had been helped a little along the way by the availability of better quality petrol and also by the introduction of self-mixing oil during 1956. No longer was it necessary to indulge in the messy addition of oil to the petrol content of the tank, or to swill the oil and petrol around in a can until it seemed to be thoroughly mixed. Garage forecourt oil dispensers followed, to make filling up with the correct ratio of petrol to oil even easier. The rider benefited because the burnt oil created fewer carbon deposits and the period between decokes doubled. Visually, it also helped diminish the trail of blue/white smoke from a two-stroke's exhaust which, until then, had to be tolerated.

As far as a rider with sporting aspirations was concerned, it was now possible to start riding in competition events at a much lower and less expensive level and, initially, at least, to do so without having to compete against experts. It was at club level that the two-stroke appeared to have the most to offer in the fifties, especially at scrambles.

The TT: once the world's greatest road race

Having lost its status as a qualifying round in the World Championship, the TT has become such an emasculated event that anyone who did not visit the Isle of Man in its heyday would have difficulty imagining just how much prestige it once held - not just in British eyes but worldwide, too. In the early days, a race win in the TT ensured overnight success for the machine's manufacturer because it had proved itself against the very best in open competition. The 37.75 mile course was considered the ultimate test of man and machine, demanding a mixture of skill, courage and determination. It was not good enough to have a machine sufficiently fast and able enough to complete the race because, in addition, the rider needed to be in peak form and possess a photographic memory, with total recall, of the course's many twists and turns: stone walls, kerb stones, telegraph poles and all the hazards of the public highway left no margin for error. Weather conditions that could vary in minutes from one part of the course to another, made high speed riding even more hazardous. If a certain machine won a TT race that was THE machine to buy, even if it bore only a passing resemblance to its over-the-counter version bore. Lessons learnt in racing were always passed on for the benefit of the customer, or so we were led to believe.

The build-up to the TT began several weeks before the races were held during early June. Every red-blooded motorcyclist was expected to regard it as one of the highlights of the year, and the two motorcycling weeklies, *The Motor Cycle* and *Motor Cycling,* did much to raise enthusiasm to fever pitch. In those days even the national dailies had motorcycling correspondents who, as well as providing gossip about the riders and details of the machines, also drew attention to the attractions of the Isle of Man as a holiday resort. The hoards of motorcyclists who descended on the Isle of Man during TT week could be sure of a genuinely warm welcome from the residents. Many of the visitors came for a fortnight, so that they could watch the practising that began a week before the races, when riders had to qualify by lapping within a pre-

scribed lap time. It also gave them time to explore the beauty of the Island before the roads that formed part of the course were closed for racing and the main purpose of their visit came about.

Getting to the Isle of Man by motorcycle in those days had a spirit of adventure about it, like a voyage into the unknown. With no motorways or roll-on/roll-off ferries, it could prove a lengthy (and often arduous) journey for those who lived in areas remote from Liverpool, the main port of embarkation. For someone who lived south of London, the first obstacle was to bypass the city centre, which meant using the North and South Circular Roads, always busy with traffic and innumerable sets of traffic lights. It was a simple and easy to remember route to follow, without need to carry a map: follow the A5 to Weston-Under-Lizard, then the A41 to Birkenhead. Progress was slow by today's standards, even on a motorcycle, but there were plenty of transport cafes at which to stop and get a cheap but wholesome meal and a welcome rest, especially if the weather was bad (as it so often was!). On arrival at Birkenhead it was merely a question of heading for the Mersey Tunnel and paying the toll, emerging from the exit signposted to Liverpool Docks. Prince's Landing Stage, from which the red and black funnelled boats for the Isle of Man sailed, was easy to find after first passing under the arches of the old Liverpool overhead railway, still in evidence during the early fifties.

The ordeal was by no means over yet. On arrival at Prince's Landing Stage the petrol tank had to be pumped out by one of the AA or RAC men on site, and a label stuck on to show this had been done. Those who had been to the TT before were familiar with this routine and arrived with an almost dry tank. It proved a rude awakening for the newcomer, however, especially if the tank had been topped up close to Liverpool. It was alleged the petrol pumped out was available on return from the Island, but most was sold to lorry owners as few claimed it on their return.

The next shock was the need to join a long, long queue in a vast, shed-like building, where fellow enthusiasts and their bikes were waiting to catch the next available boat. In theory, sailing times were given when tickets were bought in advance but, in practice, it was first come, first served. As each boat was loaded to capacity, it cast off and headed up the Mersey, whilst those who were left waited patiently for the next. There never seemed to be any arguments or trouble.

Looking back, it seems remarkable that the primitive way in which passengers were handled was tolerated. In the waiting area there were no facilities for either washing or refreshment, let alone seating. A few lavatories were deemed sufficient. As soon as a boat was ready for embarkation, it was necessary to either ride or push each solo or sidecar outfit up a slippery wooden gangplank, devoid of any side rail. If the hapless rider let the clutch in too rapidly, or if the engine stalled and the machine ran back, there was nothing - other than the stout arms of a seaman - to prevent rider or machine (or perhaps both!) from disappearing into the murky waters of the Mersey!

Prince's Landing Stage was a floating dock, so loading was not dependent on the tide. Once on board, each solo motorcycle was put on its stand (or prop stand if it didn't have one), and then roped to the machine either side of it. If it had no stand of any kind, it was leant against whatever happened to be convenient and roped to that. All were on deck, in the open and totally unprotected from the elements. If the crossing happened to be a rough one, a dousing in sea water was inevitable! The riders and their passengers sought refuge

The TT: once the world's greatest road race

The author's 1922 499cc Light Solo Sunbeam is one of three machines being off-loaded by crane at Douglas, en route to the Vintage MCC 1957 TT Rally.

in whichever lounge happened to be convenient - and prayed it would not be a rough crossing. Few could afford the luxury of a cabin for the four hour crossing, and not many the restaurant for a sitdown meal. Tea and buns provided the now much needed sustenance for the majority, after joining yet another long queue. In the event of a rough crossing, 'medical' staff (mostly women of Amazonian proportions whose appearance and ministrations would not have been out of place in a Russian prison camp) were on duty to tend to the seasick. The timid sought solace in the bar, where beer was one shilling a pint!

On arrival at Douglas the unloading saga began. Douglas harbour did not have a floating harbour, so if the tide conditions were not favourable the motorcycles had to be winched off by crane, three at a time. This in

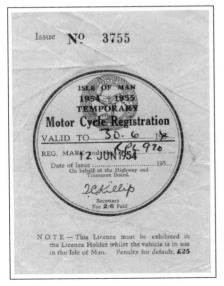

The temporary tax disc and driving licence issued to the author during his first visit to the Isle of Man TT in 1954.

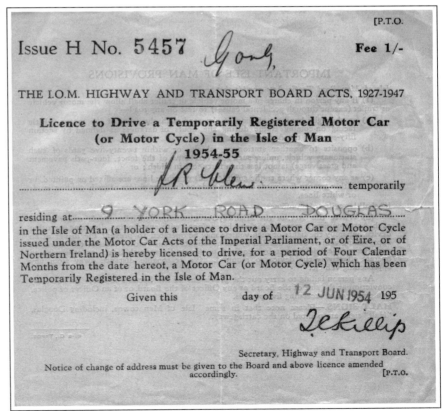

itself was a lengthy and sometimes unnerving performance, but, before riding away, the rider had first to join two more queues. Because neither the UK driving licence nor the tax disc were valid in the Isle of Man at that time, a temporary driving licence and tax disc had to be purchased from two dockside huts. Only after this final ordeal had been endured could the rider and passenger head for their lodgings, or if they had arrived in the early hours of the morning, for an early breakfast in Douglas.

One more formality needed to be attended to after arrival, the obtainment, from the steamship's office in Douglas of a so-called 'return voyage priority ticket'. This ensured there would be enough room for the motorcycle, as well as its rider and passenger, on the return sailing. Of course, it necessitated joining another queue unless requested when the tickets were booked in advance.

It's understandable to conclude that this tedious ritual would dissuade anyone from ever visiting the TT again but, strangely enough, nothing was further from the truth. A first-time crossing was invariably made with a spirit of adventure, and so keen was the anticipation of what was to follow that the many irritations soon faded into insignificance, especially after a good night's sleep. There was a certain magic about the Isle of Man at TT time and in being one of the many enthusiasts who made this annual pilgrimage to the 'promised land'. It is a feeling that has to be experienced as it's impossible to describe by words alone.

An alternative day excursion to the Isle of Man was organised by the weekly magazine *Motor Cycling*, much favoured when petrol rationing was in force and by those who could manage to wangle only one day off from work to see the TT. It involved travelling by rail and boat to watch the Lightweight and Senior Races on the Friday of TT week. Special trains departed from London, Coventry, Leeds and Leicester on the Thursday evening, with connections from other main towns and cities, before arrival in Liverpool during the small hours of the morning. The travellers then walked three-quarters of a mile to a waiting boat that took them to Douglas where, on disembarkation, they chose and walked to a convenient vantage point within a three mile radius. At 7.00pm that evening, tired and footsore, the travellers left Douglas harbour on their way back to Liverpool, to arrive at their starting point early on Saturday morning.

It was a harrowing journey, with little opportunity for sleep, but for an all-in cost of £3.5s.4d. (£3.26) who could complain? It gave many the opportunity to see the TT races for the first time, at low cost. Some years after the excursions had ceased, Graham Walker, the editor of *Motor Cycling*, was asked, off record, what he thought about these excursions. His reply was that in view of the hardship suffered, all should have been paid for the privilege of going on them!

By 1950, the TT had settled down into something like its prewar pattern, with additional races for amateur clubmen. The latter gave an aspiring road racer the opportunity to race in the Isle of Man on the cheap without coming up against the professionals and works-entered machines, and realise an ambition, to have ridden in the TT. There were four clubman races: 1000cc, Senior, Junior and Lightweight, which meant having to contain the TT programme in sixteen days, practise and all. It stretched the organising ability of the A-CU to the limit.

The pattern of the racing itself already differed from that of the prewar era,

The TT: once the world's greatest road race

and would continue to change as the years progressed. Quite apart from higher race speeds brought about by a combination of better petrol, improved front and rear suspension, better tyres and brakes, and improvements to the course itself, other factors influenced development of the road racing motorcycle.

Starting with the 500cc Senior race models, the postwar ban on superchargers eliminated Velocette's ingenious vertical twin, known as the 'Roarer'. It had not been ready in time for serious use in the 1939 Senior TT, even though it had been entered with Stanley Woods as its rider. All he was able to manage was one practise lap on it, before reverting to a 495cc single from the same factory for the remainder of practise and the race. The Roarer's potential will, for ever, remain unexplored.

The original E90 499cc AJS 'Porcupine' twin with its forward inclined cylinders was similarly handicapped, as it, too, had been designed to be supercharged. Although some subsequent redesign alleviated the problem to an extent, the edge was taken off its performance. It achieved some racing successes and won for AJS the 1949 500cc World Championship with Les Graham aboard (and nearly the 1949 TT before a sheared magneto spindle brought about its retirement), yet it never quite matched up to expectations. It is surprising the AJS management did not take a leaf out of Norton's book and produce a 500cc version of the already successful 348cc 7R much earlier than 1958, by enlarging the bore to 90mm. The resulting G50 Matchless gave the 499cc Norton a good run for its money and was a better option for short circuit races. The Matchless G45 twin was never really in the running and the G50 arrived too late.

Norton carried on more or less where it had left off in 1939, thanks to Joe Craig's continual development of the highly successful single cylinder dohc engine. Norton's superiority was reinforced by the introduction of the 'featherbed' frame in 1950, designed by Rex McCandless, a chassis that provided an entirely new dimension in roadholding. However, even with rising star, Geoff Duke, it was becoming obvious Norton was living on borrowed time, as the Italian four-cylinder multis seemed bound to gain the upper hand once their handling and reliability problems had been sorted out.

One of the first leading British riders to realise this was AJS teamster Les Graham who, in 1952, signed with MV. He was followed later by Geoff Duke, who went to Gilera. It must have been an agonising decision to make from a patriotic viewpoint alone, but it was a move that had to be made in order to remain a serious contender for the World Championships. John Surtees left Norton to join MV in 1956.

Whereas the Senior class tended to be the province of the all-conquering Norton, Velocette had the edge in the 350cc Junior. Its 348cc Mark VIII KTT carried off the 350cc World Championship honours in both 1949 and 1950, thanks to Freddie Frith and Bob Foster respectively. From this point, however, the company's fortunes foundered. Percy Goodman, the driving force behind the factory's racing effort, fell ill during 1951 and died. Although the company managed to

Norton was not afraid to experiment. This 'kneeler' was based on the conventional 348cc Manx 'featherbed' model and tried by Ray Amm during practice for the 1953 Junior TT but not ridden in the actual race. Petrol was carried in low-slung pannier fuel tanks and delivered to the carburetter by a petrol pump. The machine is now on display in the Sammy Miller Museum.

Motorcycling in the 50s

field 'works' entries in 1951 and 1952, it was a spent force, no longer able to sustain a racing development programme. At the end of 1952 the Racing Department was closed and its machines and spares sold. Velocettes were no longer 'Always in the Picture', as advertisements once proudly claimed.

Although the demise of Velocette bade well for Norton, offering them what looked like a clear run in the Junior class for the next couple of years, that company was well aware of the now imminent challenge from the Italian manufacturers. It came first from Moto Guzzi, its horizontally-engined singles showing a remarkable turn of speed and reliability. By 1953 Moto Guzzi had won its first 350cc World Championship and held it successively until 1958 when MV gained the upper hand. As a result, Norton won its last 350cc World Championship in 1952.

The 348cc 7R AJS should also have benefited from Velocette's demise. It had made its first public appearance in 1948 and initially showed great promise, especially when Geoff Murdoch rode one into 4th place in that year's Senior TT. Yet, whilst it did well in Continental race meetings, it was overshadowed in the TT by its contemporary, the 348cc Norton. A continuous development programme kept the 7R competitive, but it was not the two valve sohc 7R that won the Junior TT in 1954, AJS's only Junior TT win in the fifties. The machine ridden to victory by New Zealander, Rod Coleman, was a 'works' triple overhead camshaft three valve model, with modified bore and stroke dimensions.

From the British viewpoint, the Lightweight class was a complete disaster as the last British-made machine to win a Lightweight TT had been a New Imperial ridden by Bob Foster in 1936. After the war, British manufacturers ignored the 250cc racing class, apart, that is, from Velocette, who fielded a team of three 248cc dohc racers in 1951 and one in 1952. Virtually cut-down KTT models with changes of front fork, the racers failed to make their mark, although Bill Lomas was fifth on one in 1951 and Les Graham finished fourth on the lone 1952 entry. Benelli won the 250cc World Championship in 1950, then Moto Guzzi in 1951 and 1952, before NSU's Rennsport twins claimed it for the next three years in succession. MV then assumed prominence until the end of the decade, and was defeated only once, by Mondial, in 1957.

A Lightweight 125cc class was not included in the TT programme until 1951, before which this class of road racing had not been taken too seriously in Britain. Home-modified 123cc BSA Bantams were no match for the already well-established Italian sohc and dohc four-strokes that were winning races on the Continent at over 70mph. The Lightweight 125cc class remained the domain of

Velocette entered a lone 248cc version of its famous 348cc KTT racing model in the 1952 Lightweight TT. Les Graham is seen in the saddle of the machine on which he finished 4th To the immediate left is a happy-looking Bertie Goodman, who was then in charge of the company's racing effort.

82

the much faster Italian and German four-strokes throughout the decade. In the 125cc World Championship, the results from 1956 on were identical to those of the 250cc Championship, MV Agusta conceding only to Mondial in 1957. Until then, Mondial had won it in 1951 and 1952, MV Agusta in 1952 and NSU in 1953 and 1954.

A Sidecar race had not been included in the TT since 1925, although there had been abortive attempts at its revival in the early thirties. Sidecar races were popular in the Continental Grands Prix, Eric Oliver having won the Sidecar World Championship for Norton from 1949 to 1951, Cyril Smith in 1952 (also for Norton), and Eric again in 1953. Eventually, the A-CU relented and included a sidecar race in the 1954 TT. Run initially over the shorter Clypse Circuit, and later over the 37.75 mile Mountain Course, the Sidecar TT proved a success and has continued. Only drivers of the calibre of Eric Oliver and Cyril Smith could have kept the superiority of the Italian multis at bay with their single cylinder Nortons for so long, by inspired riding and sheer race tactics. When Oliver retired in 1955, BMW had already won its first two Sidecar World Championships and continued to do so for the remainder of the decade, and well into the next.

Clubman's races were not included in the TT programme until 1947. They were for standard road machines, bought over-the-counter and entered by the A-CU affiliated Club, of which the rider had to be a paid-up member. The machine had to conform to the maker's standard specification, a minimum of 25 having been made. It had to be started by its kickstarter, even after the compulsory pit stop. The only significant dispensations allowed the use of an open exhaust system of constant diameter, removal of the lighting equipment and the fitting of racing tyres. If desired, an air scoop to aid cooling could be fitted to the front brake.

Initially, there were only three classes: 1000cc, 350cc and 250cc, the 500s having to run in the 1000cc class. However, it soon became evident that the 1000cc class was comprised almost exclusively of 998cc Vincent vee twins, which would easily outrun a good 500. As a result, the 500s were separated out for a new 500cc class in 1949. It was also becoming apparent that Britain's only other 1000cc model, the Ariel Square Four, did not possess sufficient stamina to contest the race at the same speed as that of which a Vincent was capable. The 1000cc class developed rapidly into a Vincent benefit and in 1954 was dropped.

Initially, the most obvious choice for the 500cc class was an International Norton or a Triumph twin. The Norton was the more favoured as it handled better, even with the plunger-type rear suspension it had at that time. A Triumph spring wheel was no match, even if Ernie Lyons had used one in the wet to win the 1946 Manx Grand Prix. The picture soon changed when continuing development of the BSA Gold Star made it a fearsome competitor. Part of its success was due to some very effective gamesmanship by the BSA race personnel, who went through the Clubman's race regulations with a fine-toothed comb, to gain every possible advantage. By 1956, the 500cc Clubman's Race had become a Gold Star benefit, when BSA took the first six places. Out of the 28 finishers, 20 rode Gold Stars!

In the beginning, the 350cc class attracted several different makes, but by 1951 the majority of entrants were riding BSA Gold Stars. The advent of the 90 Plus Douglas horizontally-opposed twins heralded a brief return to racing by this greatly renowned name, when 25 were entered in the 1950 race. 12 of

Clubman races were not confined to the Isle of Man and others, sometimes of an endurance nature, were staged elsewhere. Thruxton airfield, near Andover, was well-known for its 12 hour race. Here, Bob McIntyre is seen refuelling his Royal Enfield twin in the 1954 event. (Courtesy Allan Robinson)

Motorcycling in the 50s

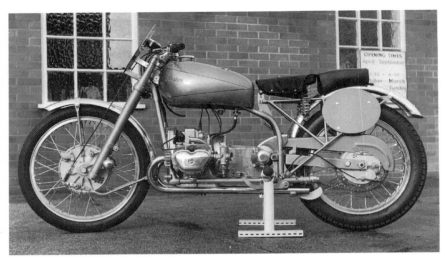

The 90 Plus 348cc Douglas had its moments of glory: no less than 25 were entered in the 1950 Junior Clubman's TT. Only 12 finished, two of which in 4th and 5th places. Sadly, they were soon overwhelmed by the Gold Star BSA, which eventually dominated both the Junior and Senior Clubman's Races.

them finished, two of them in 4th and 5th positions. There were also 14 Nortons, 6 AJSs and an EMC two-stroke amongst the finishers. A year later, the Douglas entry had fallen to 18, of which one finished 7th and two qualified for a Finishers Award. The 350cc Gold Star BSA was now in its ascendancy and, even with Freddie Dixon's help, it seemed the 90 Plus Douglas had had its brief moment of glory. As the company was still in the hands of the Official Receiver, it's remarkable it managed to achieve as much as it did. By 1956, BSA's superiority in the Junior Clubman's Race had become overwhelming: out of the 50 finishers, the first 6 rode Gold Stars and only two other makes - Norton and Velocette - were represented. Small wonder, therefore, that all the Clubman's Races were abandoned after 1956.

The 250cc Clubman's Race died an early death, due to the lack of suitable machinery. Inaugurated in 1947 along with the other classes, 1950 proved to be its last year. Its early demise was inevitable, as that year it attracted only 17 entries, of which 3 were non-starters and only 5 finished. The field comprised mainly prewar sohc Excelsiors and Triumphs, postwar but now obsolete Velocettes and a lone Panther. This class literally died on its feet because British manufacturers could offer nothing that was likely to prove competitive.

Taking a look at the international races, the mainstay of the Isle of Man TT, Norton, managed to retain its grip on the Senior Race until 1955, after which Geoff Duke on a 493cc Gilera four demonstrated the superiority of man and machine, ably backed by Reg Armstrong on a similar mount. The honour of bringing the first Norton home, into 4th position, went to Jack Brett, closely followed by Bob McIntyre on another Norton.

A glimpse of what the future held in store occurred when, during his third lap, Geoff Duke recorded an average speed of 99.97mph. At first he was credited with the first 100mph lap and it is still open to conjecture whether or not the three figure speed was achieved. An accurate measurement of the 37.75 mile course had not been made during recent years, and its realignment in places could well have shortened the racing line sufficiently to account for the difference.

From 1956 on, John Surtees, another ex-Norton rider, dominated the TT with his 'works' four-cylinder MV Agustas, with just one exception; in 1957 it was Bob McIntyre's 493cc Gilera four that took the chequered

Did he, or didn't he? Although Geoff Duke led the 1955 Senior TT from start to finish, as the leader board shows, he was credited with a record lap at 99.97mph on his Gilera. It was believed at the time that he may have recorded the first 100mph lap, as the course length had not been measured accurately for some time, despite improvements that included realignment in some places.

The TT: once the world's greatest road race

flag. He, too, had 'gone foreign'. Norton was not entirely out of the picture, however as, with one or two exceptions, at least one was amongst the first six placed men.

In the Junior TT, the pattern was much the same for the Norton riders. Although they had to face home-based competition from their AJS rivals at first, AMC acquired Norton Motors during 1952 and thereafter they raced for the same parent company, even though they retained marque autonomy. Norton's last Junior win was in 1953, as AJS managed to gain the upper hand in 1954 when the race was won by Rod Coleman. Although it was a long overdue win for the 7R AJS, Rod was riding a 'works' 7R3 version. Moto Guzzi carried off the honours for the next two years, but in 1957 Bob McIntyre's TT 'double' ensured Gilera won the Junior as well as the Senior Race. It was not until 1958 that the Junior became the province of John Surtees and the MV four. Even so, there was still spirited resistance from Norton, as well as from AJS and DKW.

As mentioned earlier, the 250cc Lightweight TT was a battleground for the Italian four-strokes, although in 1954 the German NSU twins carried all before them, taking the first four places. From 1955 onwards, MV Agusta made all the running, with riders of the calibre of Ubbiali, Colombo and Taveri. Fergus Anderson carried the flag for Moto Guzzi in 1952 and 1953. This company

Bob McIntyre (Gilera no.78) about to pass John Surtees (MV no.64) in the 1957 Senior TT. McIntyre won at 99.54mph. (Courtesy Castrol (UK) Ltd)

Motorcycling in the 50s

was always in the hunt until 1958 when it withdrew from racing.

The 125cc Lightweight TT was also fiercely contested by the Italian manufacturers. NSU upset the balance a little with a win and a fourth place in 1954, whilst the Spanish Montesa two-strokes posed a threat in 1956 by taking second, third and fourth places. MV Agusta had been the dominant force since this class began in 1951 and remained so, although Mondial never gave in until its promising star of the fifties, Tarquinio Provini, joined MV after it quit racing at the end of the 1957 season. Towards the end of the decade, MZ, Ducati and Honda were all offering MV a serious challenge - and waiting in the wings.

The re-introduction of the Sidecar TT after a lapse of almost 30 years aroused a great deal of excitement and undoubtedly tempted an even greater number of enthusiasts to visit the Island for the 1954 TT. The Sidecar Race was run over the shorter and more sinuous Clypse Course, which used only part of the Mountain Course (from Cronk-ny-Mona to Creg-ny-Baa, in the reverse direction), its total distance being just under 11 miles. It had been used for the International Lightweight 125cc Race since its inception, and was used for the International Lightweight 250cc Race and the Clubman's TT Races in 1955. Shorter races not only helped ease the pressure on the already overcrowded TT programme, but also on the local inhabitants. Practise sessions and the races themselves demanded frequent road closures, which placed restrictions on freedom of travel.

The 1954 Sidecar TT proved an easy win for Eric Oliver and his passenger, Les Nutt, on their 499cc Norton/Watsonian outfit. They were so far ahead on their last lap that they virtually toured home to victory. Their outfit was both low and fully streamlined, paving the way for the 'kneeler' outfits that would soon follow. The BMW outfits of Hillebrand, Noll and Schneider took the next three places. It was a foretaste of what was to follow as, in 1954, the Sidecar World Championship was won by Noll and the year following by his teammate Schneider, Eric Oliver having retired at the end of the 1954 season. From then on, a BMW sidecar outfit won every Sidecar TT until the end of the decade, although not without strong challenges from Norton drivers such as Cyril Smith, Australian Bob Mitchell and Jackie Beeton, to name but three.

Over the ten year period, the TT had both its bright and darker moments. The highlight of the decade had been the Golden Jubilee TT of 1957, the last occasion on which the 'works' teams of that era were fully represented. Ironically, Norton, who was to celebrate its own Golden Jubilee later that year, had withdrawn

John Hartle tended to be underrated despite the fact that he achieved some very good results on a number of different machines. He was 2nd on an MV four in the 1959 Junior TT and 2nd in the following year's Senior Race. (Courtesy: Allan Robinson)

The TT: once the world's greatest road race

support for racing at the end of the 1956 season. Joe Craig had retired a year earlier and from that point on policy had been to race only the type of machine supplied to private owners, without streamling. The factory relented enough to permit its 'works' machines to be entered unofficially for the Golden Jubilee TT, with streamlining, if desired. Three riders received sponsorship to take advantage of this offer: Jack Brett (Lord Montagu), John Hartle (Eric Bowers) and Alan Trow (Reg Dearden). Of the three, only Trow finished in both races, although Brett put in a lap at 97.5mph on one of the legendary 90 bore models, before he came off on the 7th lap. Bob McIntyre was the hero of the Golden Jubilee TT when, on a 493cc Gilera four, he recorded the first official 100mph lap in the Senior Race. Four laps were over the three figure mark, the fastest of which was 101.12mph.

Two other incidents involving the Golden Jubilee TT are also worthy of mention. Much to everyone's surprise and delight, veteran Stanley Woods turned out on one of the early morning practise sessions to ride a 349cc Moto Guzzi. 18 years had passed since his last ride in the TT, his re-appearance being the result of a carefully hatched plot between himself and *Motor Cycling*, intended to form the basis of a feature in that magazine. Despite his age disadvantage, the long gap since his retirement from racing, and his unfamiliarity with the machine, he showed he had lost none of his old skills, completing a lap of the Mountain Course at just under 80mph and, after turning out again during an evening practise session, was rewarded with a final lap at an average of 82mph!

Also present at the TT that year was Rem Fowler, who had won the twin cylinder class in the first TT of 1907 on a Norton. Wisely, he kept both feet firmly on the ground, in deference to his age.

Eric Oliver, passengered by Stan Dibben, was persuaded out of retirement for a lap of honour, to drive his 1954 Norton/Watsonian outfit around the 37.75 mile Mountain Course whilst the roads were closed. Never able to resist a challenge, Eric and Stan averaged a surprising 73.62mph, to the delight of the onlookers.

It was not all good news, unfortunately. Charlie Salt lost his life during the last lap of the Senior Race. He was one of several who died in the Isle of Man TT during the fifties, amongst them the popular and very likeable Les Graham in the 1953 TT. Ironically, he had won his first TT for MV only the day before. Others lost their lives whilst contesting the European Grands Prix, including Fergus Anderson, and amongst the Commonwealth riders, Ray Amm, another who left Norton to sign up for MV Agusta.

In 1958, three of the leading Italian manufacturers - Moto Guzzi, Gilera and Mondial - decided to withdraw from racing. Development expenses and the overall cost of running a racing team had got out of hand, the machines themselves having little, if anything, in common with standard production models. Moto Guzzi, for example, had been experimenting with an in-line four and had even raced a vee-eight in the Golden Jubilee Senior Race. MV Agusta carried on much as before, now with greatly reduced opposition. Adopting a curious form of subterfuge, MV continued to race factory-entered machines supported by mechanics from the factory race shop, with a label marked 'Privat' stuck on the fuel tank! It fooled no-one and lost that company a great deal of respect.

What happened to Geoff Duke? A good question to ask at this juncture. He had been suspended by the FIM for the first half of 1956 whilst the reigning

Rem Fowler, winner of the Twin Cylinder Class of the first TT in 1907, is greeted by the Mayor of Douglas in 1957, the TT's Golden Jubilee year. The machine is a replica of the Peugeot-engined Norton twin on which Rem won the 1907 race.

Motorcycling in the 50s

Some famous names find time to share a joke during the official opening of the Montagu Motor Museum at Beaulieu on 5th April 1959. Left to right: Geoff Duke, Harold Daniell, Hugh Viney and Jock West.

1955 500cc World Champion. His 'crime' had been to support the private runners during the 1955 Dutch Grand Prix, who rode only one slow opening lap before pulling in to retire, in order to draw attention to the fact that they were underpaid. Geoff was one of 13 professional riders who sympathised with them and took part in this dramatic protest. All were suspended for six months. He rode for Gilera again in 1957 but, when they withdrew from racing a year later, changed allegiance to a 500cc BMW and rode his own 350cc Norton, with little success. For 1959 he rode his own 350cc and 500cc Nortons and agreed to ride a 250cc Benelli in the Swiss Grand Prix. In one day he won all three races with all three machines! It proved a fitting grand finale for one of Britain's greatest ever riders, for this was his last race. He retired quietly, with grace, still able to beat the best.

John Surtees, his greatest rival, continued with MV Agusta until the end of the 1960 season, when again he was crowned 350cc and 500cc World Champion. During the season he had been racing cars as well, taking second place in the British Grand Prix at Silverstone, driving a Lotus 18-Climax 4. From 1961 on, he deserted motorcycling completely and transferred so successfully to four wheels that, in 1964, he became World Champion whilst driving for Ferrari. He was the first motorcyclist ever to hold a World Championship title on four, as well as two, wheels. It was a remarkable achievement that did much for British prestige.

The withdrawal of support for racing by many of the leading manufacturers did not portend well for the TT, or, for that matter, motorcycle racing in general. However, fears for the future were soon dispelled, as other manufacturers began to take the place of those who had dropped out. The whole scene changed quite dramatically when the Japanese began to show their potential, after a humble beginning.

Riding styles changed, too, as did the attitude of riders. As speeds rose still higher, the dangers of racing in the Isle of Man seemed to become more apparent to the vociferous few, including leading riders of the day who should have known better. All of this compounded so that in the fullness of time the TT lost its status as a World Championship qualifying event. Exactly how it happened is a long and sad, yet intriguing, story of its own.

The bubble that burst

For quite a long time there had been only two ways in which a motorcyclist could carry a passenger - by having the passenger ride pillion or attaching a sidecar. Whilst the sidecar provided by far the more comfortable option of the two, to acquire and fit one represented quite a heavy financial outlay, assuming the machine to which it was to be fitted was suitable. The majority of riders opted for the pillion seat, which was already fitted to a number of machines, together with footrests, as part of the overall specification. Even if they had to be purchased and fitted separately, the cost was relatively small in comparison to fitting a sidecar.

Unfortunately, the pillion seat provided by most manufacturers was no more than a small slab of sorbo rubber covered in leathercloth, bolted to the rear mudguard. It did little to absorb any road shocks, especially when fitted to a rigid frame bike. It rightly deserved the cynical description of 'an upholstered brick'. It was, of course, possible to buy proprietary pillion seats of the sprung mattress or pneumatic type which offered a better level of comfort. These were a trifle more expensive, though, so many riders tended not to buy them, especially if the more basic type was already fitted. Not having ridden on their own pillion seat, riders had no idea how uncomfortable it could be! The real answer came when the dualseat arrived - but only if the machine had a spring frame - and it was soon adopted as the standard fitting on all spring frame models.

The other problem associated with pillion riding was that, although the rider shielded the passenger from the worst of the weather, it could still be very uncomfortable. Some manufacturers, such as Veloce Limited, fitted a two-level dualseat to its machines so that the pillion passenger had good vision over the rider's head. When the weather was bad, however, it made it even more difficult for the passenger to shelter behind the rider's back. Because the rider needed to be alert all the time, there was always something to occupy the mind, whereas the passenger had no such distractions and was more con-

Motorcycling in the 50s

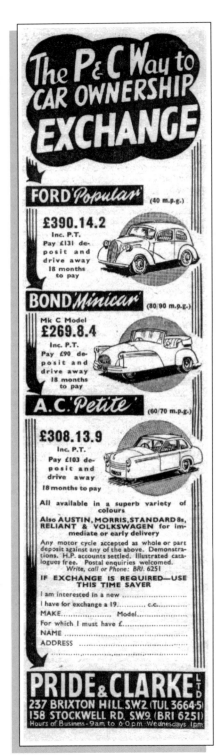

scious of feeling either wet or cold and sometimes a combination of both.

The sidecar had its advantages (and also its disadvantages), as outlined in the next chapter. To many, a more acceptable alternative became available in the early fifties, the so-called minicar or 'bubble car' as it was commonly later called. Today's use of the word microcar seems more appropriate. The bubble car offered much higher levels of comfort without the need to dress up specially, and allowed a civilised conversation to be held rather than a few shouted words. If there were young children, it was possible to carry them, too, in some of the models, together with a moderate amount of luggage. Many were, however, both slow and noisy internally.

The first microcar appeared at the 1949 Motor Cycle Show. With one wheel at the front and two at the rear, the Bond Minicar was designed by Lawrence Bond, an aircraft engineer, and made under license by Sharps Commercials Ltd of Preston, Lancashire. Its power unit was a 122cc Villiers 10D single cylinder two-stroke engine, built in unit with a three-speed gearbox.

Appearance-wise, the early Bond Minicar had little to commend it as resembled a fairground dodgem when viewed from the front. Built extensively of light alloy, its greatest advantages were not just its price (£203.16s.6d.), but also its lightness in weight. Because it had no reverse gear, it had to be lifted at the rear to turn it round in a confined space. However, this lack of a reverse gear meant it could be driven on a Group III (motorcycle) driving licence, obviating the need to take a car driving test. Despite having such a diminutive engine, its lightness in weight gave the Bond Minicar a favourable power to weight ratio. It was capable of speeds in excess of 40mph and would carry three people across its bench-type seat in relative comfort. Depending on loading, it was also quite feasible to achieve 100mpg fuel consumption.

The forward-mounted engine and gearbox unit was attached to a centrally-positioned front steering fork assembly, pivoted at the top and bottom of the steering head, from which it drove the front wheel by chain. The steering fork assembly took the form of massive L33 aluminium alloy castings, its movement controlled by an enclosed spring suspension unit aided by a Hartford friction-type shock absorber. Steering and starting were somewhat unsophisticated, the former relying on adjustable steel cables passing around a bobbin on the end of the steering column. The engine was started by a floor-mounted hand lever attached by heavy gauge cable to another lever on the splined shaft, where the kickstarter would have been attached to the engine unit. A sharp pull back would suffice to start it. A cranked lever protruded through the dashboard to provide a dashboard-mounted gearchange. It was connected to rocking levers on the gearchange shaft of the gearbox by adjustable Bowden cables.

Pride & Clarke could supply not only microcars but also the Ford Popular and several other family cars on its familiar 'easy terms'. In 1954, on payment of one third of the purchase price you could sign the agreement and drive away. You then had to pay the balance (plus interest) in eighteen equal monthly instalments; an arrangement often referred to as 'paying on the glad and sorry' - glad I've got your car but sorry I can't pay for it!

The bodywork was built on the stressed skin principle, the Minicar having no chassis. 18 gauge hard aluminium sheet was used in its construction, with the main transverse bulkhead in 14 gauge alloy. There was no suspension at the rear, nor was there a differential or a rear axle. What little insulation there was from road shocks came solely from the 16 x 4 inch Goodyear tyres, fitted to stub axles.

All three wheels were of the same size, and had split rims to make tyre changing easy. Brakes - of the internal expanding type, operated by rod and cable - were fitted to the rear wheels only. The brake, clutch and accelerator pedals were floor-mounted, and there was a steering wheel like that of a conventional car. The parking brake was of the 'walking stick' type under the dashboard.

Weather protection was provided by a generous windscreen fitted with a single wiper and detachable sidescreens. A canvas hood folded across the rear of the vehicle, and was so easy to put up it was claimed it could be fitted whilst the Minicar was in motion. Although there was no boot, there was a large luggage locker behind the seat which, it was claimed, would stow all the gear needed for a fortnight's holiday.

A flywheel magneto on the Villiers engine provided the ignition and 6 volt lighting, controlled by an ignition and lighting switch on the dashboard. Twin headlamps mounted either side of the bodywork, just to the rear of the bonnet, were considered adequate for normal driving after dark. An accelerator pedal acted as a throttle in the conventional manner, and a choke lever protruded through the dashboard. The only instrument was a speedometer, belt driven from the front wheel.

The great thing about the Bond was that it was so cheap to run and cost less than the average sidecar outfit. The road tax was the same as that for a sidecar outfit (£5 per annum), and insurance was cheap in view of the small capacity engine.

A contemporary road test involved a 233 mile drive from Preston to London by two 11 stone men, carrying an additional 7 stone of luggage. Although it must have been a tedious journey, taking just over 10 hours, the economy aspect was only too apparent. Petrol consumption averaged 97mpg, and the average speed was 22.8mph.

Despite its appearance and lack of sophistication in certain respects, the Bond Minicar proved remarkably successful and continued to sell over a long period of time. Its specification was constantly upgraded, so that by 1952 it had a more powerful 197cc Villiers engine, a more positive steering system and a much more attractive body with mouldings in fibreglass. There was even a Minitruck and a Minivan, later followed by a three-door hatchback estate.

It was not until 1952 that other microcars began to appear, one of which not only looked odd but also had an unusual name - the Workers Playtime! Made by The Electrical Engineering Construction Company Limited of Totnes, Devon, it had two wheels at the front and one at the rear, its curvaceous lines and compact size accentuated by a two-tone finish that gave a first impression of a three-wheel sidecar. It was built on an all-steel electrically welded chassis, with bodywork of box section construction, the front of which lifted upwards to give access to the seat.

The prototype was powered by a 246cc Excelsior twin cylinder two-stroke engine, but later this was changed in favour of a 322cc British Anzani twin. It is alleged it derived its curious name in recognition of a workers playtime broadcast by the BBC from the factory premises.

Somewhat heavy in weight at 5.5

Comerfords, the well-known motorcycle dealer at Thames Ditton in Surrey, was another that diversified into microcars, as this 1956 advertisement shows very clearly. It, too, would take a motorcycle (or car) in part-exchange.

Motorcycling in the 50s

As time progressed, the overall appearance of the Bond changed dramatically, as this nicely-restored 1956 Mark D shows. It is seen regularly at rallies and similar events in and around Somerset, driven by Janet Clark. (Courtesy Norman Bown)

cwt, and uninviting in appearance, it is not known how many were made - none seem to have survived. When details were first announced it was expected to retail at £280 plus Purchase Tax, but the performance characteristics of the Excelsior-engined prototype were not in its favour. Petroil consumption was around only 55mpg and the maximum cruising speed 37mph. Judging from the publicity photograph and the vehicle's stated width of four feet, it would accommodate just one passenger of average build on the bench-type seat.

The AC Petite appeared at the 1952 Motor Cycle Show, another with a single wheel at the front and little or no pretension of styling. The engine was a 346cc Villiers 29B single cylinder two-stroke mounted in the boot, which drove a Burman gearbox through a triple belt and pulley arrangement, providing three forward speeds and reverse. Of only 8 inch diameter and fitted with a 4 inch section tyre, the front wheel was mounted on a trailing link fork, controlled by coil springs and a hydraulic damper. The rear wheels were of 18 inch diameter and shod with 3.25 inch section tyres, independently sprung and with a car-type differential. They were driven by chain final drive. Other features included a self-starter, a roll-back soft top roof and a bench-type front seat which would carry two adults or one adult and two children. This layout necessitated column gearchange. Made by one of Britain's oldest car manufacturers - A.C. Cars Ltd. of High Street, Thames Ditton, Surrey - it was priced at £398.3s.4d.

With three different microcars on the market, it would be interesting to know what initial effect they had on the motorcycle trade and how many were sold from the time the Bond made its first appearance in 1949 to the end of 1952. Unfortunately, the industry's statistics are not sufficiently broken down to provide this information, because the broad heading 'three wheelers' also includes sidecar outfits and the Reliant three-wheeler.

More a full-blown three-wheel car in its own right, the Reliant was fitted with a car-type four cylinder water-cooled 750cc engine, based on the old Austin 7 engine of similar capacity. For these reasons alone the Reliant does not come within the definition of a microcar and is therefore excluded from this survey. This may explain its long-lasting appeal and why it is still in production today, having undergone many changes to ensure it remained a viable alternative to the conventional and more expensive four-wheel car and the sidecar outfit.

The market remained more or less unchanged throughout 1953, but towards the end of 1954 a newcomer with stylish bodywork appeared on the market, the Allard Clipper. Already famous for his sports cars and having won the Monte Carlo Rally in one of them, Sydney Allard formed The Allard Clipper Company in Fulham Road, London SW6 to make and market his latest innovation. By using fibreglass, the car's bodywork could be moulded in complex shapes with flowing lines, breaking away from the 'dodgem' or lack-lustre designs of others who were limited by using sheet metal. Additional advantages of fibreglass lay in its lightness in weight and structural strength and freedom from corrosion.

Adopting the single front wheel and two rear wheels layout, the Clipper's chassis was of channel section steel, with a motorcycle-type steering head to accommodate an alloy single-sided front fork. The trailing arm of the fork had a stub axle for mounting the front wheel, its movement controlled by a Andre vane-type rubber in compression unit. Each rear wheel was also mounted on a trailing arm that terminated in a stub axle, and used a similar Andre unit to control its movement. There was no differential. All three wheels had Lockheed hydraulic brakes.

The engine unit was a fan-cooled 346cc Villiers 28B single cylinder two-stroke, air ducts in the bodywork providing additional cooling. It was mounted inside the bodywork in front of the nearside rear wheel, which it drove by chain via a three-speed and reverse Burman gearbox. Like the AC Petite, the primary drive was by triple pulleys and vee belts. The Wipac electrical equipment included a self-starter and a windscreen wiper, with power for the 6 volt lighting circuit from the engine's flywheel magneto. The front wings were moulded in so that the driver did not easily realise the Clipper had only three wheels. It was the wheels, however, that completely spoilt the overall appearance of the Clipper. Of only 8 inches in diameter and shod with 4 inch section balloon tyres, they seemed out of proportion; far too small in size. Spoiling otherwise enterprising styling, they gave the Clipper an odd, unbalanced look.

Described as a two- or three-seater coupe, the Clipper sported a single bench seat for its occupants and a hard top with a wrap-around windscreen. There was a door on the passenger side only. To keep the interior completely weatherproof, sidescreens were available as optional extras to fully enclose the hard top.

An unusual feature that had long since disappeared from cars was the way in which the rearward-opening boot could be converted (for an additional charge) into a dickey seat, to carry two children. The words "in comfort" were used; an optimistic statement if ever there was one! The children had only minimal protection from the weather, were isolated from their parents and would be more aware of the noise from the engine that was in close proximity, no matter how well it was shielded by the partition behind the bench seat. Also in the boot were hazards posed by the 2.5 gallon petroil tank and battery.

At the 1954 Motor Cycle Show the Clipper was priced at £267.15s. It was claimed it would sustain a speed of 40mph and return a fuel consumption of approximately 70mpg. It was never road tested by *Motor Cycling* like most of its contemporaries, and although it was still listed at the time of the 1955 Motor Cycle Show with the same specification and at the same price, by the time of the 1956 Show the Clipper had disappeared completely.

Although the motorcycling press had not raised the issue at the time, it is obvious little thought had been given to how well a microcar would withstand a collision and what protection (if any) it would afford its occupants. Admittedly, traffic density was much less than it is today, and the average speed of vehicles lower. Yet, taking the case of the Allard Clipper as an example, placing children outside the main body of the vehicle, close to a fuel tank without a protective bulkhead or firewall, was tempting fate. Was this taken into account by a prospective purchaser?

MESSERSCHMITT CABIN SCOOTER

MODERN MOTORING with CAR COMFORT AND MOTOR CYCLE ECONOMY

KR 200 THREE-SEATER

Motorcycling in the 50s

Nothing quite like the Messerschmitt Kabinenroller had been seen before and it was this design, more than any other, that gave rise to the term 'bubble car' on account of the transparent plastic dome that enclosed both driver and passenger. Perhaps due to its unusual appearance or price, it sold in the UK in only relatively small numbers; the KR200 model cost just over £340. (Courtesy Norman Bown)

It was left to Germany to present a totally different concept of the bubble car when the Messerschmitt Kabinenroller (Cabin Scooter) was imported during April 1954. Quite unlike anything seen before, it was made by the company that had produced military aircraft during World War 2. The Kabinenroller had its two wheels at the front and in overall appearance resembled an aircraft shorn of its wings and tail unit, the effect being heightened by the seating of the driver and passenger in tandem with a transparent cover above their heads. Indeed, some of the less well-informed seemed to think it was a means of using up surplus aircraft assemblies! A totally designed package, it kept the factory open and the Messerschmitt soon established a good reputation for its reliability and handling, and for the quality of its build. It seems probable it was the appearance of the Messerschmitt that first gave rise to the use of the word 'bubble car' as a descriptive term for these cars.

Imported by the Beulah Hill Engineering Co., Ltd. of London, SE19, the Messerschmitt had 8 inch diameter wheels with 4 inch section tyres (like those of the Allard Clipper), although, in this instance, they complemented the design rather than detracted from it. The slim bodywork, with its built-in twin headlamps and integral wings for the front wheels, was of pressed steel, attached to a welded, duplex tubular frame. The front wheels were mounted on independently sprung rocking arms controlled by a graduated rubber spring. At the rear, a sub-frame carried the fan-cooled 174cc Sachs single cylinder two-stroke engine and its four-speed gearbox. It was of the pivoted fork type, its movement controlled in a similar manner to that at the front. The engine had a Siba 12 volt electrical system provided by the flywheel, which performed the roles of dynamo, electric starter and, on switching, a reverse gear.

Seating was provided by car-type seats in tandem, the driver steering by a pair of handlebars that had a twist grip throttle on the left in lieu of an accelerator pedal. The steering was direct. The positive stop gearchange lever was on the right of the driver's seat and there was also a ratchet handbrake. Floor-mounted pedals controlled the clutch and brakes in conventional car fashion. Access was gained by raising the canopy to the right, where it was restrained by a leather strap.

A road test carried out by *Motor Cycling* in December 1954 was highly complimentary, the only criticisms being slightly hard suspension and engine noise. Handling was first class due to the narrow track and long wheelbase, and the top speed in the region of 55mph. Fuel consumption averaged 90mpg - even when maintaining 50mph for long periods. The K170 Kabinenroller cost £335.18s.2d.

Two larger capacity (191cc) KR200 models were soon added: the Standard and the de Luxe, both of which contained provision for carrying an adult and a child at the rear. It was also possible to have the KR175 models fitted with an ingeniously modified Siba Dynastart, included in the specification of the KR200s. By persuading the Sachs two-stroke engine to run backwards, it provided a reverse gear without need to modify the gearbox. Other minor modifications made to the KR200s included a curved windscreen and car-type control layout. Perhaps surprisingly, the Messerschmitt was not too common a sight on our roads.

The unusual seating arrangement of the Messerschmitt gave rise to speculation about what might happen if one of these vehicles was used for taking a driving test and the brakes were applied with gusto during the emergency stop!. With the test instructor sitting behind the driver it was quite possible for him to be forced out of his seat and up over the driver's head, ending upside down with his face in front of the driver's.

Bubble cars gave rise to a host of cartoons, one of which portrayed an RAF type in a Bond, complete with handlebar moustache, firing a machine gun mounted on the bonnet. In front was a Messerschmitt with black smoke pouring from it, its driver crouched over the controls and glancing fearfully over his shoulder!

Some bubble car manufacturers seemed to find it difficult to come up with both an attractive design and a transmission system that was really practical. When the Gordon made its debut at the 1954 Show, it seemed as though neither of these two factors had received a great deal of attention. Having a solid-looking appearance that was more in keeping with that of the Reliant, the engine/gear unit appeared to have been added almost as an afterthought. Furthermore, it drove only the rear right-hand wheel by chain! One can only conjecture how effective this would have been when carrying an overweight passenger on a bumpy road!

The Gordon, made by Vernon Industries Ltd. of Admin Road, Kirkby Trading Estate, Liverpool, had its good points, too. Adhering to the one wheel at the front layout favoured by British manufacturers, the wheels were of 15 inch diameter and fitted with 5.20 inch section tyres. They helped give the car the solid 'full-size' look, far removed from that of the adult 'toy' and its minuscule wheels. A backbone ran from the steering head of the front wheel to the rear of the car, with crossmembers serving as supports for the engine/gear unit and the bodywork. Front suspension was by a hydraulically-damped motorcycle-type leading link fork. The rear wheels were carried by a swaged crossmember and attached to trailing arms controlled by hydraulically-damped coil springs. Of the 'open' type, the body had a folding canvas hood for use in bad weather, and transparent side curtains. The single bench seat would accommodate the driver and a passenger, with the option of two additional hammock seats behind it (standard on the de Luxe version).

Unfortunately, the whole effect was spoilt by the location of the engine, which was on the *outside* of the car, where the driver's door would normally be, partially enclosed by a fairing with a large, oval cooling vent in the front. It gave the car an unbalanced, lopsided appearance, spoiling the look of what otherwise would have been acceptable bodywork. A Villiers 197cc single cylinder two-stroke engine provided the motive power with an integral three-speed gearbox that had a reverse gear. Although an electric starter was included in the specification, the kickstarter had been retained for emergency use. Final drive was by a heavy duty chain to the offside rear wheel.

By the time the Gordon went into production, a number of changes in specification had been made. The standard model retailed at £269.17s.9d.

and the de Luxe version at £285.15s.11d. Production ceased during August 1957, by which time just under 2000 had been made.

The next German design to appear on the UK market was the Fuldamobile, powered by a 199cc Sachs single cylinder two-stroke engine, and in some ways reminiscent of the Allard Clipper. Yet, although it used the same size wheels as the Clipper, the styling was a much better compromise as the wheels blended in and were far less obtrusive. Unfortunately, the high price of the Fuldamobile (£429.12s. for the standard NWF200 model and £448.11s.5d. for the de Luxe) put it out of contention. After just seven months it was no longer imported by the Beauship Trading Co., Ltd. of 25, Savage Gardens, London EC3.who had acted as its UK concessionaire.

Another short-lived newcomer was the German-made Bruetsch, two versions of which were made in the UK under licence by Bruetsch Cars England of Sherwin Road, Castle Boulevard, Nottingham. These cars deserve mention because they were so appealing in appearance, although anything less like a bubble car is difficult to imagine. The two-piece fibreglass body lent itself exceptionally well to sports car styling, especially with the two-in-the front and one-at-the-rear wheel layout, the wheels being of 4.00 x 8 inch (199cc) and 4.00 x 12 inch (247cc) diameter. A simple 'T' type chassis was used, with ingenious diaphragm-type rubber suspension. The two versions were powered respectively by a 191cc and a 247cc Ilo single cylinder two-stroke engine. Their respective retail prices of £325 and £395 did not seem unreasonable in relation to the quality of the build, so why they never went into production is not known.

A year later in 1956, the importation of a quite different Breutsch was announced, the 50cc Mopetta, a single-seat three-wheeler powered by an Ilo single cylinder two-stroke engine. Designed to carry two persons seated in tandem and with twist grip throttle handlebars, it was vastly different in appearance to its predecessors, having its single wheel at the front. It was to be sold in the UK by Automotive and Marine Ltd. of The Crown Garage, Albany Street, London, SW1 for £207. Claimed to have a maximum speed of 32mph, it could also boast fuel consumption of no less than 150mpg. The full specification included a windscreen wiper, flashing indicators and even a heater. However, it, too, seems to have suffered a similar fate to that of the larger capacity models.

The two wheels at the front layout seemed to lend itself more readily to bodywork styling, as became apparent when another British newcomer - the Powerdrive - arrived on the market towards the end of 1956. The single wheel at the front seemed to emphasise the fact that the vehicle was only a three-wheeler, whereas when there were two wheels at the front it was nothing like so evident. The Powerdrive was the first really attractive British design, giving the initial impression of a full-size sports car. More to the point, this appearance was performance-related, as the fan-cooled 322cc British Anzani twin cylinder two-stroke engine fitted was quite vigorous, having a rotary valve incorporated in its crankshaft assembly. Located in the boot with the three-speed and reverse Burman gearbox, it drove the rear wheel by chain and had a Siba Dynastart starter-generator.

Described by *The Motor Cycle* as "one of the world's most elegant three-wheelers", the Powerdrive had a chassis of the space frame type of welded, tubular structure. Independently sprung, the two front wheels were attached to a leading arm and movement was controlled by a motorcycle-type shock absorber. The rear wheel was mounted on a trailing arm, its movement controlled in a similar manner. 5.30 x 13 inch wheels fitted with hydraulic brakes helped create the impression of a big car, as did the fact that two adults and a child could be accommodated on the bench seat, with storage for luggage both in the nose and at the rear. The Powerdrive cost £412.12s.7d. and was distributed through Blue Star Garages. Despite the addition of a later Mark II 2-3 seater tourer in late November, followed by a Mark III version with improved suspension in August the following year, it did not sell anything like as well as might have been expected. Production had ceased by February 1957 with only 360 of the Mark II and III versions sold.

From Holland came yet another short-lived microcar, the 197cc Hostaco Saloonette. Imported by the Progress Supreme Co. of 852, Brighton Road, Purley, Surrey (who had better success with the Progress scooter), its distinction was in the use of a doorless, all-polyester plastics body, in which the 197cc engine was mounted behind the seats. It drove the 4.50 x 10 inch single rear wheel by chain, via a three-speed and reverse gearbox. It appears to have been a lively performer with a quoted top speed of 56mph, and sold for just under £400.

The next significant contributions - the 245cc BMW Isetta and the 174cc Heinkel Cabin Cruiser - came from Germany. Both of these were four strokes. Built along somewhat similar lines, bodywise, with a roll-top roof, both had a rear-mounted fan-cooled engine and a front-opening door that gave access to a bench seat for two, with left-hand drive, a layout which lent itself well to having the two wheels at the front.

The BMW Isetta came first, when UK imports commenced in April 1955. This, however, was the four-wheel version with twin rear wheels in close proximity to each other. (It was not until September 1958 that two three-wheel versions were imported: the 300 Standard Saloon and the 300 Plus Saloon, both two-seaters fitted with an uprated 298cc ohv single cylinder engine of the company's own design and manufacture). Fan-cooled, it drove the single rear wheel by a fully enclosed chain through a four-speed and reverse gearbox. Like the quality of the build, the specification was just as enterprising: independent front wheel suspension with 10 x 4.8 inch tyres and a 10 x 5.2 inch rear tyre, all three wheels with hydraulic brakes. The engine had an electric starter and there was a 12 volt lighting system. The wheelbase was 4 feet 10 inches and the track 3 feet 11.5 inches.

The 300 Plus version had the luxury of a heater, separate head and sidelights, front and rear bumpers and an external mirror. Two months later, an automatic version of both models became available, its Selectoshift transmission giving two pedal control

The BMW Isetta was powered by an updated 245cc version of BMW's prewar single cylinder four-stroke motorcycle engine. This right-hand drive version was made in Brighton, Sussex by Isetta Great Britain Limited, a company set up by BMW to handle the manufacture and sale of microcars in Britain. The CD registration number prefix confirms this car was first registered in Brighton. (Courtesy Allan Robinson)

Motorcycling in the 50s

The Heinkel (like the BMW Isetta) was first imported from Germany, as evidenced by the left-hand drive. It was possible to get two adults and two small children within its confined space, although all needed to be good friends! (Courtesy Allan Robinson)

with a clutchless gearchange.

BMW marketed its cars not through its UK motorcycle concessionaire, AFN of Isleworth, but through a new company, Isetta of Great Britain Ltd, New England Street, Brighton, Sussex. The Isetta Standard retailed at £339.19s.6d. and the Isetta Plus at £365.19.6d. They were available with a whole range of extras, such as a spare wheel and tyre, luggage carrier etc.

The Heinkel Cabin Cruiser - the product of another wartime aircraft manufacturer - was first imported in June 1956, initial imports coming direct from Germany and later ones from Eire. Its specification and bodywork were broadly similar to the Isetta, although on the Heinkel only the two front wheels had hydraulic brakes. The tyre sizes were 10 x 4.4 inches. Heinkel fitted their own 174cc ohv engine until February 1958, after which it was uprated to 204cc by increasing the bore size. When imports from Eire commenced, it was reduced slightly to 198cc. Longer and fractionally wider than the BMW, the Heinkel had a wheelbase of 5 feet 8.75 inches and a track of 3 feet 11.75 inches. Having only the one model priced at £403.6s.6d., the Heinkel Cabin Cruiser was imported by International Sales Ltd. of 34/40, Palfrey Place, London SW8. Later, the Heinkel was built in Croydon, Surrey, as the Trojan.

The BMW Isetta and the Heinkel Trojan proved quite popular and large numbers of each were seen on the road. They, too, became the butt of bubble car cartoons: One showed a BMW and a Heinkel in head-on collision with the enraged driver in each shaking his fist and shouting "Just you wait until I can get out!"

Other British-made designs, such as the Berkeley, Coronet, Frisky, Nobel and Scootacar, came and went towards the end of the decade. The Berkeley and the Coronet were both of the two wheels in the front type and powered by a 328cc Excelsior twin cylinder two-stroke engine. In the Berkeley (which looked like a sports car) it drove the front wheels and was air-cooled, and in the Coronet it drove the single rear wheel and was fan-cooled. Both had attractive, stylish bodywork, especially the Berkeley, but they arrived on the market a shade too late and remained in production for little more than a year. The Frisky lasted a little more than two years after three changes of engine specification, starting with a 9E 197cc fan-cooled Villiers engine and ending with a 328cc Excelsior twin, but even its Italian-styled fibreglass bodywork failed to save it from obscurity.

The Nobel, powered by a 191cc Ilo single cylinder two-stroke engine, failed to make much impression and only just over 400 were sold during its first year on the market. As for the Scootacar, it, too, used a 197cc 9E 197cc fan-cooled Villiers engine. Made by Scootacars Ltd. of 125, Jack Lane, Leeds 10, it merits description on account of its unusual design and construction. Of the two wheels at the front type, the engine was fitted at the rear, driving the single rear wheel via a four-speed gearbox. The front independent suspension was coil spring; the rear comprising a single-sided pivoted fork arrangement controlled by an Armstrong shock absorber unit. The wheels were of 8 inch diameter and fitted with 4 inch section tyres. It had an exceptionally strong chassis of welded box section steel covered with a sheet steel floor.

The fibreglass bodywork gave it an odd, chunky appearance, broad at the bottom and tapering to a much smaller width at the top. The seating arrangement was very unusual, too, taking the form of a longitudinal squab which abutted a bench seat across the rear to form a letter 'T' configuration. The driver sat astride the squab, having only a padded backrest similar to that of a

The Heinkel was later sold in Britain by Trojan, who had premises in Croydon, Surrey. As can be seen, the Trojan name was prominently displayed on the three-wheeler's front-opening door. (Courtesy Allan Robinson)

typist's chair. The passenger sat in the centre of the rear bench seat, legs astride the squab, as there was no gap in it. It was also possible to accommodate two small children on the rear seat, one either side of the passenger, a large door on the nearside providing access to all. The foot controls were similar to those of a car but, in place of a steering wheel, there was a scooter-type handlebar. The electrics were 12 volt and included an electric starter and windscreen wiper. It cost £297.10s.

There were a few other microcars made during this period, such as the Tourette, which seemed only to appear in surveys of what was available and not at the 1958 or 1960 Motor Cycle Shows. Others were almost ghost-like and, if they did appear at all, only very few were made.

The microcar went on into the sixties but not for long. Now that Britain was coming out of a period of austerity, there was more money to spend and a cheap secondhand car became a better proposition. However good a compromise the microcar had been, its disadvantages were becoming more and more apparent: it was not particularly comfortable, did not have a good enough performance and, in many cases, was so noisy inside that normal conversation was not as easy as might be imagined. Luggage also created problems in some, unless it could be slung on an external carrier. The Scootacar would have been one of many microcars that encompassed all these problems.

Competition existed also in the form of four-wheel microcars, miniature cars in the true sense, like the Goggomobil, although it was not until the end of the decade that a far more serious threat arose from the new Austin and Morris cars. The world-famous Mini had arrived, launched by BMC in August 1959. Retailing at fractionally under £500 inclusive of Purchase Tax, the Mini, with its transverse-mounted four-cylinder engine, integral gearbox, clutch, differential and transmission that took up only 18 inches of body space, was a clear pointer to what lay ahead. It carried four people in comfort with ample space for a reasonable amount of luggage, was easy to drive and park on account of its small size and embodied an exciting new concept. Just as its predecessor, Herbert Austin's Austin 7, had heralded the decline in popularity of the sidecar when it was announced in 1922, so the ubiquitous Mini brought down the curtain on the microcar.

Today, a fifties microcar has become a collectable item, some of the rarer survivors in good condition fetching considerable sums of money that can go well into five figures. Not very practical in today's traffic, they have become a curiosity rather than the novelty they once were, just like their forebear, the cyclecar, which enjoyed a similar brief spell of popularity just before and immediately after the 1914-18 war - and suffered a similar fate.

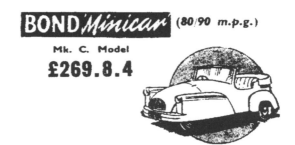

BOND *Minicar* (80/90 m.p.g.)

Mk. C. Model

£269.8.4

Whatever happened to the sidecar?

There has existed the need for a motorcycle to accommodate a passenger ever since they became powerful enough to carry two people. All manner of methods were tried during the pioneering days, ranging from the attachment of a trailer to the rear of a solo motorcycle to a seat in the front of what was known as a forecar. The latter took the form of a tricycle with its wheels arranged so that its single wheel was at the rear end with a seat placed between the two front wheels, in which a forward-facing passenger could be seated in front of the driver. Neither approach proved very satisfactory ...

The person seated in the trailer (usually a girlfriend or the rider's wife) became enveloped in the clouds of dust that were kicked up behind the machine as it chugged its way along the unmade roads of that time. If it was wet the dust turned into a mixture of mud and water. The oil discharged from the machine's exhaust also blew rearwards and, as horses were commonplace in those days, their droppings were despatched in this direction when disturbed. Many a promising romance ended abruptly when the dirty and bedraggled passenger climbed out of the trailer at the end of a journey; assuming the trailer was still attached to the motorcycle towing it, that is! It was not unknown for a trailer connection to break unnoticed by the rider, who carried on, blissfully unaware of what had happened. If a trailer did become detached it would flip over backwards, most likely depositing the, by now, hysterical passenger in a muddy ditch filled with stinging nettles!

The forecar was a no more satisfactory alternative because, not only did the hapless passenger act as a weather break for the driver, but also had the dubious benefit of a grandstand view of any impending accident. The only remaining option would have been to carry the long-suffering passenger on a cushion strapped to the rear carrier; hardly the acme of comfort! Small wonder, then, that the sidecar outfit came into its own.

The sidecar made its first tentative debut around 1901, but some years were to pass before it attained general acceptance. Generally speaking, side-

Motorcycling in the 50s

car drivers fell into two categories: those who were really enthusiastic and could handle a third wheel with dexterity, and those who fitted a sidecar out of sufferance. The latter group usually comprised those who owned more sporting types of machines, perhaps someone with a young family who needed the means with which to take his wife and children on holiday, or on longish journeys, at comparatively low cost. The outfit more than likely had to be used for commuting to and from work, too. If lucky, the machine already owned would be suitable for hauling a sidecar after fitment of a smaller engine sprocket to lower the overall gear ratios, plus any other necessary minor changes. If not, the beloved machine had to be changed for something more suitable.

Some riders became sidecar converts and thereafter favoured driving an outfit. Under adverse conditions, and especially in ice and snow, a sidecar outfit is the safest vehicle on the road, a fact reflected in the cost of insurance premiums, which were substantially reduced whenever a sidecar was permanently attached. Unfortunately, part of this advantage was lost because road tax increased if a third wheel was added.

Statistically, sidecar outfits were included with tricycles under the broad heading 'three-wheelers', as is still the case today. It therefore becomes difficult to plot the popularity of the sidecar on a year-by-year basis. In the twenties the cheap light car would have accounted for a drop in sales, especially after Herbert Austin announced his Austin 7 in 1922, which went into full scale production a year later. The car sold for £225 (at a time when a good quality big twin sidecar outfit was between only £40 and £60 less) and brought popular motoring a step closer for the man in the street. Even so, it has been estimated by sidecar enthusiasts that, in 1936, about 125,000 sidecar outfits were in use and that, before the outbreak of war in 1939, one third of all motorcycles on the road had a sidecar of some kind attached .

A surprisingly large number were of the commercial type; little more than a large capacity box on a sidecar chassis with a rear-mounted drop tail that would act as a loading ramp. These were favoured by tradesmen such as window cleaners, sweeps and plumbers, and by motorcycle dealers who used them to transport solo motorcycles or to collect spare parts from stockists. Some were even used for fire-fighting, carrying all the hoses, extinguishers and pumps on a platform whilst, in the USA, a particularly bizarre application was an iron-barred cage fitted to the chassis which the police used for transporting a prisoner!

Although there had been an abundance of ex-War Department motorcycles for sale soon after the end of World War 2, this did not apply to sidecars. In comparison to solos, the armed forces used relatively few, which would have been of little use to the civilian market in any case. Heavy in weight, the bodywork was made of wood and had seating only for one, offering virtually no protection from the elements other than a raised protective shield at the front. Behind the seat was a box-like locker, presumably for carrying ammunition. The sidecars were made with fittings for a 596cc Norton 'Big Four' and had provision for sidecar wheel drive from the machine's rear wheel through a short propellor shaft.

Sidecar manufacturers resumed business as soon as possible after the war, although they, like motorcycle manufacturers, experienced continual problems with the supply of raw materials. At this time the bodywork was still built along traditional coachbuilding lines, comprising a wooden framework to which metal panels were attached. The bodywork was suspended on semi-elliptical leaf springs with the wheel fitting on a stub axle attached directly to the chassis.

Six British and one German manufacturer exhibited at the 1951 Motor Cycle Show, offering, between them, almost 50 different kinds of body. There were also four motorcycle manufacturers who listed their own-branded sidecars, which may - or may not - have been made on their own premises. The seven manufacturers were Blacknell, Garrard, Laxton, Matheson, Steib (from Germany), Swallow and Watsonian. Garrard's new Silchester single-seater saloon had a dynamo resembling a brake drum attached to the sidecar wheel, which kept a Lucas 20amp/ hour battery charged so that the luxury of a heater and radio could be included in the overall specification. At the time of the show, the arrangement was still in the experimental stage, but it was anticipated the sidecar - so equipped - would be available in 1952. Garrard continued to make its ever-popular commercial box sidecar, as did Watsonian, who had a wider variety of styles.

It was by no means unusual to see a sidecar attached to a lightweight motorcycle, carrying a passenger or for commercial use. The Garrard Gazelle catered for this type of user, having a lightweight design suitable for attachment to a machine within the 125-200cc range. The Swallow Gadabout was initially supplied with a small, box-type sidecar and even the Corgi was available with a similar, miniaturised attachment that banked in unison with the motorcycle. There had even been several tandem bicycles powered by a clip-on cyclemotor attached to an ultra-lightweight sidecar. Mum and Dad rode on the bicycle whilst Junior was carried in the bicycle-type sidecar!

Although sidecar driving necessitates a different technique to that used

Although Claude Rye Ltd sold everything that related to motorcycles, it did not specialise in sidecar (a few other dealers did). Even so, the company claims in this 1954 advertisement an impressive display of 200 sidecars at its Fulham Road premises.

Busmar Limited of Blackpool tended to specialise more in family sidecars and produced some pretty impressive double adult designs that seemed almost to overwhelm any machine to which they were attached.

Motorcycling in the 50s

Business or pleasure!

The neat and highly mobile Berkeley Caravette helps you to lead two lives — and makes both of them more pleasant. As a business trailer for the local trader it is a smart little van with a useful capacity. For weekends or holidays it becomes a luxurious camper-caravan, with sleeping accommodation for two adults and a child. A detachable cooking unit is included. To add to the covered space, specially designed extension tents are available. Any reasonably powerful motor-cycle combination — or any small car — will tow the Caravette comfortably, smoothly, safely and economically. Powerful brakes are fitted. Another extra of special interest to small-holders, market gardeners and other country dwellers is the open truck body. It is interchangeable with the normal body and can be switched over in a few minutes. Caravette complete with sprung interior mattresses, furnishings and cooking unit

	£99.15.0.
End extension tent	£11.17.6.
Side extension tent	£11.17.6.
Open truck body	£15. 0.0.

For further details write for an illustrated folder, to Berkeley Coachwork (Sales & Export) Ltd., Biggleswade, Bedfordshire.

It's easy going in the BERKELEY CARAVETTE

Berkeley Caravette behind the latest BSA motor cycle combination.

Berkeley produced the Caravette which could legally be towed behind a sidecar outfit. The Caravette was claimed to accommodate two adults and a child, which suggests it must have been very cramped inside and hardly suitable for a rainy holiday! A detachable cooking unit was included and extension tents were available (and probably needed!).

Already underpowered and subject to a host of problems arising from poor quality control, the mere thought of adding a single-seat sidecar to the Brockhouse-made Indian Brave beggars belief! No doubt those who purchased such an outfit have an interesting tale to tell ...

when riding solo, it is quite easy to master by following a few simple guidelines. There are other, more obvious, minor problems, such as having to re-adjust for width, being able to correctly judge when parking close to a kerb, and having to revise braking distances. Very few sidecar outfits had a reverse gear so parking in places with difficult access had to be avoided: a heavily-laden outfit is difficult to manhandle unaided.

How well an oufit would handle on the road depended very much on how well the sidecar was attached to the machine. Opinions varied as to whether there should be three or four connections, with four seeming to have the majority vote. The three essential components comprised a swan neck that located with a lug cast in or bolted to the motorcycle's front down tube, a straight connection with an adjustable end that located with a lug on the main down tube under the saddle or dualseat, and a ball joint in the vicinity of the rear wheel spindle. Any machine regarded by its manufacturer of being capable of hauling a sidecar would invariably have cast-in lugs on the frame as connection points but, even if there were none - such as in the case of a lightweight machine - clamp-on fittings could be purchased. It took skill, care and experience to line up a sidecar chassis, but, if done correctly, it made a world of difference. Some individuals seemed blissfully unaware of this and often one would see a motorcycle leaning drunkenly towards the sidecar and know instinctively it was a pig to handle. There were a number of dealers who specialised in supplying and fitting sidecars whose advice - based on long experience - could prove very beneficial.

The choice of machine was virtually unlimited, although, more often than not, it was a case of using what was already owned. When needing to make a choice of machine, however, some preferred a sidevalve single with its legendary low speed torque. Others, who needed better performance, opted for an ohv or ohc single, or a vertical twin. With the exception of the Vincent, the once very popular vee-twin was no longer available postwar. This is one of the reasons Watsonian considered making its own motorcycle powered by a vee-twin JAP engine. This idea came to nothing, though, for reasons described elsewhere.

When scooters began to become popular the market opened up for sidecars to fit them. Both Vespa and Lambretta offered own-branded sidecars, and even a trailer, in the case of the former company. Other sidecar manufacturers such as Blacknell and Steib followed suit. Not all were for passenger carrying; commercial sidecars were popular, too. One was made to look like a loaf of bread, its crusty top in the form of a lid that could be raised. Douglas Vespa became the recipient of a Royal Warrant for supplying a Vespa and box sidecar to HRH Prince Philip, the Duke of Edinburgh. Though there is no record of whether he ever drove it, it's known to have been used for transporting his equipment when playing polo.

Some companies specialised in making just bodies and others in making the chassis. Amongst the bodymakers were Rankin and Trinder, whilst Greeves could supply a chassis. Not everyone exhibited at the annual Motor Cycle Show, which could prove expensive. At the 1952 show only Bowser, OEC and Surrey were represented.

Not everyone had room at home to keep a sidecar outfit under cover, or with access from front to rear yard. The sidecar manufacturers were well aware of these problems, one solution to which was the long-selling Watsonian Quick-Fit chassis, which could be fitted to almost all that company's models. It took experts 30 seconds to detach such a sidecar and most owners about ten minutes.

At the 1952 Motor Cycle Show. Canterbury joined the ranks of exhibitors.

BSA could offer a choice of two sidecars; a single-seat de luxe tourer or a family outfit suitable for an adult and teenager, or two smaller children seated in tandem. (Courtesy Norton Motors (1993) Ltd)

Motorcycling in the 50s

Left: Norton had only this single-seat sidecar, mounted on what was described as a double triangulated chassis. It was built along conventional lines and best suited to the sidevalve or single cylinder ohv models. (Courtesy Norton Motors (1993) Ltd)

Below: The scooter boom and development of fibreglass reinforced plastics led to some very attractive-looking scooter outfits. (Courtesy Allan Robinson)

MODEL
car, havi
Water-ti
locker w
hood and
as stand
NORTON

Below: The Blacknell double adult sidecar, mounted on a Safety Chassis, had nice lines and, unlike some of its contemporaries, did not seem to completely overwhelm the machine to which it was attached. (Courtesy Mrs Joyce Miller)

This marked the beginning of the sprung wheel chassis, one of which was displayed on the Canterbury stand. This version featured a pivoted trailing arm which carried the wheel, its movement controlled by a Girling shock absorber unit. Swallow introduced the Viscount double adult sidecar at the same time, which had bodywork of the razor edge type. Although this type of styling may have appealed then, it must have been the very devil to paint satisfactorily as paint has a natural tendency to either thin at the

Whatever happened to the sidecar?

edge or else build up a fat lip.

By 1954 a sprung sidecar wheel was becoming the norm and a trend towards the sidecar wheel brake was becoming evident, too, as in Blacknell's Safety Chassis. Blacknell, Busmar and Watsonian had lightweight sidecars to offer: the Blacknell Snug was built along monocoque lines with a 16 inch wheel and a weight of just 95lbs. Garrard could offer the ultimate in sprung sidecar wheels by listing a chassis fitted with a Clamil spring wheel or proprietary manufacture. Still a very popular design was the Swallow Jet 80, an all-steel welded and very elegant sports sidecar which had been on the market since 1949. The ranks of those who supplied bodywork only were swelled by the addition of companies like Castle, Hillsborough and Nicholson, whilst Waverley made both bodies and chassis.

Hillsborough and Noxal made an appearance at the 1954 Motor Cycle Show, the latter company having its Airflow single-seater make its debut there.

Eric Oliver, four times World Champion Sidecar Driver, drove a standard Norton Dominator twin attached to a Watsonian Monaco sidecar in the 1958 Sidecar TT. His passenger, Pat Wise, was seated normally throughout the race and they surprised everyone by finishing in 10th position, at a race average just over 13mph below that of the winner on a 'works' BMW. A one-off venture after Eric's retirement from racing, Watsonian benefited from the resultant publicity, which underlined the strength of the sidecar's bodywork.

Built along aircraft lines and of aerodynamic shape, its secret lay in its construction from shaped manganese alloy panels, welded together and strengthened internally by spot-welded ribs. Having no chassis, weight was as little as 62lbs.

The most outstanding sidecar, however, was the new Watsonian Monaco, a sports single-seater of monocoque construction with a full-width wheel hub. The wheel was suspended on a trailing arm, controlled by an Armstrong hydraulically-damped suspension unit. The show exhibit was panelled in light alloy but when the Monaco went into production the bodywork was moulded in fibreglass, like that of the Jet 80. In 1958, Eric Oliver, four times World Champion Sidecar Driver, drove, in that year's Isle of Man TT, a standard Norton Dominator twin to which was attached a Watsonian Monaco sidecar. With Pat Wise, his lady passenger, seated normally, they finished tenth; a quite remarkable feat. It gave Watsonian and the Monaco all the publicity needed and reaffirmed the structural strength of fibreglass bodywork.

For 1955 Busmar dispensed with the conventional sidecar nose when it launched its new Astral model. Egg-shaped in profile, the sidecar could accommodate an adult in the front and two children in the rear. It had large windows and a windscreen and was supplied in a two-tone finish. Canterbury offered the reverse with its giant Carmobile: two adults and one child! The Carmobile had a very wide door and twin windscreen wipers. Steib now entered the fray with a two-seat saloon which placed the passengers in tandem with a Plexiglass canopy above like that of a bubble car. Swallow went in for bright finishes and two more sidecar manufacturers - CM and Raven - had by now appeared.

The sidecar manufacturers now directed attention toward the use of fibre-

glass mouldings in place of the more traditional materials of construction; an area in which Watsonian had already taken the lead, continuing with the Bambi scooter sidecar. Towards the end of the decade, Watsonian launched its Oxford double adult sidecar, which was made entirely of fibreglass. This, however, proved a case of too much too soon. Priced at £137.10s it was expensive and, it is alleged, only a small number were sold. Steib was paying special attention to the sidecar wheel brake and could supply one that was hydraulically operated. More interest was also shown in monocoque construction which could, in certain circumstances, dispense with the need for a separate chassis: Swallow's Mark II Jet 80 and Garrard's Grand Prix were two good examples of the way in which development was heading.

It was, however, Surrey Sidecars that sprang one of the biggest surprises when it launched the Syvan two-berth caravan sidecar in late 1956! Mounted on a sidecar-type chassis, the Syvan broke new ground. It bristled with a number of ingenuous and unusual innovations and became the centre of attention for sidecar enthusiasts at the 1956 Motor Cycle Show. To set it up it was first necessary to withdraw a bolt from the wheel assembly so that the wheel and mudguard could be pivoted in the horizontal plane. This provided sufficient clearance for the left-hand side of the body to be swung outward to form an extension of the floor. A hinged panel that was originally the upper end could then be folded to re-form the left-hand side. The next stage was to support the floor area by jacks stowed underneath the floor. The canopy - which had to be lifted off before the left-hand side was folded outward - could then be raised on telescopic steel struts, one at each corner of the body. It was provided with windows and, when raised, gave over six feet of headroom. The sides were formed by canvas sheets attached to the canopy which could be secured by press studs. Suddenly there was a small-size home for two!

The basic caravan could be purchased for £139 and, for an extra £9, would come fully equipped. The extras included two air beds, a folding table and two metal frame canvas chairs, a cooking stove and plastic cups and plates. There was also an interior light. Just how many were sold is not known as none was seen on the road, but Surrey Sidecars deserved full marks for ingenuity.

Canterbury Sidecars was another publicity-seeking company to come up with the unexpected when it announced the Canterbury Belle in late 1959. Rudge had marketed a sidecar-carrying, sixteen foot long canoe in 1925, which was held to the chassis by quick-release clamps so that it could be used on the water. Canterbury, however, went one better. The boat was about the same length as the average sidecar, secured by integral lugs to the chassis by eight winged bolts. A miniature two-seater, the pram dinghy was powered by a fan-cooled 80cc JAP single cylinder, two-stroke engine and equipped with a twin blade screw, rudder and anchor. It weighed 112lbs and cost £175, inclusive of Purchase Tax. More a PR gimmick than a practical proposition, it is doubtful any were actually sold. The sight of a well-known tester from *The Motor Cycle* sinking fast caused great mirth amongst his watching colleagues!

New names were still adding to the list of sidecar manufacturers. Amongst them were Clarendon Fairings, Streamline Sidecars Limited, and Wessex Sidecars Limited, whilst it must be remembered that some of the larger London dealers, such as Pride and Clarke and Claude Rye, were able to offer their own-branded sidecars at very competitive prices. Quite a few amateur enthusiasts made their own sidecar bodies, too, a not too difficult task when building one along traditional lines with a wooden frame and metal panels. Some quite

PANTHER IN 1956

presentable designs resulted, as well as some positive horrors!

Interest continued at a high level until about the middle of the sixties when a marked decline set in. The sidecar was on its way out, the victim of the cheap, popular and often secondhand car, plus new-found affluence as the country emerged from what had seemed to be a never-ending period of austerity. Although sidecars enjoyed a mini-boom in the seventies, their pattern of use had changed and it was only the diehard enthusiasts that now bought and used them in any significant number. Today, they are nothing like so numerous on our roads; most of the modern motorcycle manufacturers do not recommend fitting them.

So far, no reference has been made to the role played by sidecars in motorcycle sport, in which Canterbury, Garrard and Watsonian all played a part. In trials, a modified road-going sidecar had been used originally, which led to the development of the purpose-built trials sidecar. It allowed the passenger more freedom to move about, so that weight could be placed where it was most needed in a tricky, observed section. There was sufficient enthusiasm amongst sidecar drivers for sidecars only trials to be organised, the best known of which was the D.K. Mansell, a trade-supported event. In later years a British Sidecar Trials Championship was introduced, at a time when the Lightweight two-stroke trials outfit was very much in the ascendancy.

Although the inclusion of a sidecar race in a scramble is by no means a new idea, it was not until 1959 that they were included in the programme of some of the larger International events such as the Sunbeam Point to Point and the Hants Grand National. It goes without saying that a sidecar (and its passenger) has to withstand a much greater pounding than in a trial, so that a different type of sidecar had to be used. Little more than a platform on a chassis, it had a variety of handholds and padded areas for the more agile passenger. Eventually, the chassis no longer bolted on and, instead, became part of the motorcycle frame to ensure absolute rigidity of mounting. In recent years, sidecar only scrambles have been run and there are British and European Scrambles Sidecar Championships.

Much the same applies to sidecars used in grasstrack racing where the passenger has to be just as agile. Early postwar outfits had a bolt-on sidecar

Where's the trapeze? This array of tubes on a grasstrack racing sidecar was once a common sight at most meetings. The photo was taken at Brands Hatch during its early postwar grasstrack days before the track was covered in tarmac to provide today's road racing circuit. Both driver and passenger are wearing the inevitable assortment of ex-WD clothing which was acceptable by the ACU at a time when few better alternatives were available.

that was little more than a chassis with a small platform and a scaffolding-like assortment of tubes to act as hand and footholds for the passenger. Current fashion dictates the sidecar is today an integral part of the motorcycle frame and has the sidecar wheel sharply inclined inwards at the top at an acute angle, like those used in sidecar speedway racing. There are 500cc and 1000cc British Championships for grasstrack sidecars.

Motorcycling in the 50s

The RAC (and AA) patrolmen with their sidecar outfits were once a familiar and often welcome sight on our roads. The RAC always favoured a Norton, the sidecar carrying sufficient tools and spare parts to get most broken-down vehicles going again, assuming, of course, that the owner was a member of the organisation. Here, an RAC patrolman uses an ordnance survey map to put the sidecar driver and his passenger on the right road at a site just off the Dorking, Surrey by-pass. Both the patrolman and the sidecar driver are setting a good example by wearing safety helmets. (Courtesy The Royal Automobile Club)

In road racing, the re-introduction of a sidecar race into the 1954 TT programme created great excitement, especially as there had been a sidecar race included in many of the postwar Continental Grands Prix. The winner, Eric Oliver partnered by Les Nutt, used a fully streamlined Norton 'kneeler' outfit developed from the 'Flying Fish' solo 'kneeler' on which Eric and Ray Amm had established a number of world records at Montlhery during the previous year. Having the advantage of a lower centre of gravity due to the rider's kneeling position and a consequently reduced frontal area, the outfit set a new trend, becoming a common sight in road racing events, later to develop into an integral unit where the sidecar became part of the motorcycle frame. It was yet another trend that would have a profound affect on the future development of the racing sidecar outfit.

AA and RAC motorcycle patrolmen were once a familiar sight on our roads. Many members who subscribed were rescued after a roadside breakdown by their respective organisation, the patrolman's commodious commercial sidecar carrying a host of tools, spare parts, a first-aid kit and a fire extinguisher to cope with most kinds of emergency. The AA favoured a BSA M21 sidevalve single to power their outfits, whereas the RAC remained faithful to a single cylinder ohv Norton. They were the true ambassadors of the road, out in all weathers, and we were all glad to see them when we were stranded. It was never the same when they went over to four wheels and the roadside boxes - from which they used to receive directions from control centre - disappeared.

Something different

Apart from the early 1900s, when Britain had less motorcycle engineering of its own to offer, foreign motorcycles were never very popular. A brief interest in the American big twins waned when the government introduced an import tariff in 1911 in order to restrict the number being imported. Apart from this exception, it was widely accepted that Britain produced the best, a notion seemingly proved by the supply of British-made motorcycles to virtually every country in the world, including Japan. Of the machines made on the Continent, a large number fitted proprietary engines and gearboxes of British manufacture.

Immediately after the war there was no possibility of bringing in foreign-made motorcycles, even if there had been the demand. Quite apart from an enforced restriction on imports as Britain struggled to earn as much as it could from exports to help repay the massive wartime debts, the Continental manufacturers were busy rebuilding their shattered industry. When they eventually did resume production they had first to meet the demand of their home markets.

Statistics provided by the British Motorcycle Industry show imports of foreign-made motorcycles re-commenced in 1952, although three foreign motorcycle manufacturers did exhibit at the first postwar Motor Cycle Show in 1948. All three makes displayed came from Czechoslovakia: the CZ, the Ogar (the latter being the forerunner of the Jawa twin) and the Manet, and it was clearly stated they were not available in Britain. CZ was there again at the 1949 show, this time with only Jawa (Manet was no longer to be found), but still neither marque was available in this country.

During late 1951, BMW reappeared on the market, the only foreign make represented at that year's Motor Cycle Show. Trading on the sensational Senior TT win in 1939, the offering was the R25/2 250cc single and three horizontally-opposed twins, the 490cc R51/3, and the 590cc R67/2 and R68. The last was a sports model with a high-level, two-into-one exhaust system and a twin leading shoe front brake. The unmistakable BMW quality was evident in them all: the shaft final drive, the plunger rear suspension and the lustrous black finish.

Listed as being available in Britain but not at the show, were four models from Moto Guzzi, one of them a scooter, imported by 'works' rider Bob Foster of Parkstone, Dorset. The 65cc Moto Leggera, the 250cc Airone Sport and the 500cc Falcone were particularly attractive in their bright red finish but, unfortunately, the two larger capacity models were more expensive than their British counterparts, at £205 and £305 respectively.

The Indian displayed at the show could not be classed an import, as the 248cc Brave, with its single cylinder sidevalve engine, was made by Brockhouse Engineering of Southport. The original American manufacturer was no longer in business and Brockhouse had by then acquired the name.

There can be little doubt that those who visited the Continental shows at this time found many of the exhibits both stylish and attractive. Although the emphasis was invariably on machines of up to 200cc capacity, their manufacturers were not afraid to experiment and break away from traditional design, nor were they hesitant to use bright colours. The only point in question was the permanence of some of these models? Only too often a promising design would disappear after the show without trace. The idea of a concept vehicle is not new, and no doubt many of the models that fell into this category were there to test public opinion. If nothing else, they showed that manufacturers were not content to rest on their laurels and were keen to explore new frontiers. Many British visitors were impressed by this approach and the desire to create something quite different that would add a bit of colour to an otherwise rather stereotyped scene.

By 1952 the British motorcycle industry had caught up with home market demand and a seller's market no longer prevailed. Over 39,000 people turned up on the opening day of the 1952 Motor Cycle Show, some 4000 more than on opening day the year before. BMW was again the sole foreign exhibitor, displaying the four model range shown the year before. Possibly EMC could just about qualify as a foreign exhibitor, since Dr Josef Erlich's 125RR road racing model was fitted with a 125cc Puch split single two-stroke engine.

Bob Foster continued to represent Moto Guzzi interests (as well as other makes) in Britain with the same four model range, although Moto Guzzi refrained from exhibiting at the show.

By the end of 1952, a total of just 1600 motorcycles had been imported, but imports rose to a total of 2400 in 1953, swelled in the main by the influx of mopeds and scooters beginning to arrive from the Continent. From the motorcyclist's viewpoint, it was still necessary to look outside the annual Motor Cycle Show to find foreign-made motorcycles, with the exception of the Vincent stand at that year's show.

Having already agreed to distribute the NSU Quickly moped in Britain, Vincent went a stage further and agreed also to assemble and market as NSU-Vincents two larger capacity NSU models, its 98cc ohv and 123cc two-stroke Fox models. By using a minimum of 51% of British-made components in assembly, Vincent could just escape having to pay import duty. It was a good idea in principle, but as sales never matched up to expectations, the arrangement was terminated after little more than a year. It was as well that costings showed it would not have been profitable to make an Anglicised version of the Max, too, as was at one time contemplated. The collapse of the arrangement was a prelude to what was to follow, as financial problems put Vincent out of business in early 1956.

DMW could also have been included as a British company with a Continental link, in view of its intention to fit a range of ohv engines made in France by Ateliers Mechanique du Centre. It had been forced into this decision when Villiers refused to supply the new 2T twin cylinder engine/ gear unit. To show this move was no idle threat, DMW had on display at the 1953 show four AMC-engined models, including the Cortina that, until then, had always been fitted with a Villiers engine. Particularly attractive was the dohc 125cc Hornet production racer, resplendent in its pale blue finish with an Earles-type front fork. Villiers got the message and relented so the Anglo-French venture failed to materialise.

Although not at the show, Moto Guzzi machines were still being imported. BMW appeared to have halted imports as it was no longer listed in the buyer's guides published by the motorcycling press.

Imports in 1954 more than quadrupled to almost 11,000, as evidenced by the appearance of more new foreign exhibitors at the 1954 Motor Cycle Show. They comprised the Hungarian-made Csepel and Montesa from Spain. Jawa-CZ reappeared, too, after winning the International Trophy in the 1954 International Six Days Trial. Now for sale in the UK and represented by Industria (London) Limited of 34, Lime Street, London EC3, the highlight of its display was one of the 248cc models actually ridden in the ISDT. The three road models - the 148cc Junior and 248cc Favorit singles and the 344cc twin cylinder Senior, all two-strokes, - were tastefully finished in red.

Csepel displayed three 247cc de Luxe single cylinder two-stroke models, built along British lines but lacking the usual European flair. Good features were full-width hubs, a duplex tube frame, and pivoted fork rear suspension. Not displayed, but listed, was a 123cc single cylinder two-stroke. No prices were available, but the UK concessionaire was Lamet Trading Limited of Plantation House, Rood Lane, London EC1.

Montesa had shown promise in the Lightweight 125 TTs of 1951 and 1954, having a surprising turn of speed yet an uncanny quietness. It was a good opportunity to introduce its three two-stroke-engined 124cc

It is alleged that when Villiers Engineering told DMW it could not supply the new 2T twin cylinder engines, DMW threatened to use instead French-made AMC engines. Villiers capitulated and DMW continued to use its engines.

Jawa/CZ machines from Czechoslovakia were one of the first postwar imports. Stylish in appearance, they also had the advantage of a competitive price structure as they were subsidised by the East German government. Competition successes in the ISDT helped, too.

THE MOTORCYCLES OF THE FIVE CONTINENTS

JAWA 250-350

Motorcycling in the 50s

Touring-Sports Model 500 c.c.-24 H.P. **BMW R 51/3**

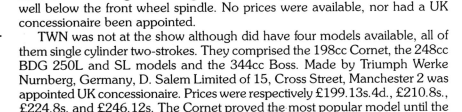

BMW assumed greater prominence in this country after the war. The characteristic black and white finish was of a high standard and introduction of the Series 3 range, with plunger-type rear suspension, helped boost sales. The company had its own sidecars, too.

models onto the UK market; the Brio 80, 90 and Sprint. Their distinguishing feature was the length of the legs of the telescopic front fork, which extended well below the front wheel spindle. No prices were available, nor had a UK concessionaire been appointed.

TWN was not at the show although did have four models available, all of them single cylinder two-strokes. They comprised the 198cc Cornet, the 248cc BDG 250L and SL models and the 344cc Boss. Made by Triumph Werke Nurnberg, Germany, D. Salem Limited of 15, Cross Street, Manchester 2 was appointed UK concessionaire. Prices were respectively £199.13s.4d., £210.8s., £224.8s. and £246.12s. The Cornet proved the most popular model until the entire range was dropped and replaced by two scooters from the same manufacturer. This happened later, after a new concessionaire had been appointed.

Moto Guzzi machines were no longer listed as being available in the UK, but BMW imports had resumed to feature two new Series 3 models, the 245cc R25/3 single and the 490cc R51/3 twin, alongside the R67/2 and the R68 as listed previously.

In 1955, imports increased by almost a factor of six over the high figure of the previous year. This staggeringly large rise came about because the scooter boom was peaking and the purpose-built moped showing its superiority over the clip-on cyclemotor. Even so, it gave cause for alarm, as British exports totalled only 800 more - 59,900 compared to 60,700. Strangely enough, the British motorcycle industry seemed to be not over-concerned, as a large percentage of the imports were of small capacity models, whereas its strength lay in the bigger machines. The industry underestimated the power of brand loyalty and their own dealers, who fought for any fast-moving machines and got their machines, service and profit from the importers, who were also more adventurous in their promotion methods.

Towards the end of 1955, more foreign manufacturers made an appearance at the Motor Cycle Show. One of the 500cc racing fours drew the crowds to Gilera's stand, providing the first opportunity for visitors to get anywhere near one. Whilst not for sale, displayed were two overhead valve models: the 150cc Sport single and 304cc twin. Gilera was unable to quote any prices as it did not have a UK distributor, which probably explained the reason for being there.

The arrangement with Vincent having collapsed, NSU now exhibited under its own name and offered two models, the 247cc ohc Max with unusual operation of its valve gear, and the newly-introduced 123cc ohc Super Fox. Both had a spine-type frame and a four-speed gearbox - and that unmistakable Continental styling. The Max was worthy of special attention as, unlike other models in which the overhead camshaft was driven by bevels or a chain, it used a system of long 'connecting rods' and eccentrics, located within a tunnel cast in the cylinder barrel. It was not an entirely new idea as W.O. Bentley had used a somewhat similar arrangement in one of his earlier car engines. Only the Max was listed in the buyer's guides at £243.3s. It proved a popular machine with a good performance, finished in an attractive blue colour.

Ambassador Motor Cycles had already arrived at an arrangement with Zundapp, the German motorcycle manufacturer, to act as UK outlet for its Bella scooters, and had displayed a KS601 Zundapp 597cc horizontally-opposed twin on its stand at the 1954 show. The possibility of importing the latter never materialised but, instead, Ambassador decided the 200S 199cc two-stroke single would offer a better proposition. Imports had commenced during October but no price had been fixed. It proved a wise decision, because the 200S and its later 201S Earles-type fork version sold well in the years that followed, offering a serious challenge to the short-lived but somewhat similar TWN.

Although the BMW 590cc R67/3 twin was now available, the model that

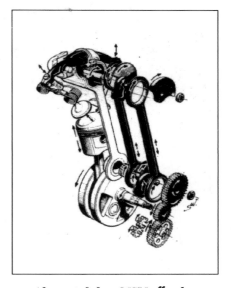

Above & below: NSU offered an entirely new approach to design, its 247cc ohv Max model having a spine-type frame and a unit-construction engine in which the valve gear was operated by eccentric connecting rods. It had a maximum speed of 78mph: better than that of many British 350s.

attracted most attention was the new 590cc R69 twin, which came to be regarded as a classic model of that era. The other two models making up the display were the 245cc R25/3 single and the 490cc R50 twin that replaced the discontinued R51/3. BMW remained faithful to the horizontally-opposed cylinder layout in the case of the twins, and all models featured shaft drive and rear suspension; plunger type on the two Series 3 models and pivoted fork on the R50 and R69.

Czechoslovakia was represented as usual by CZ and Jawa. These two

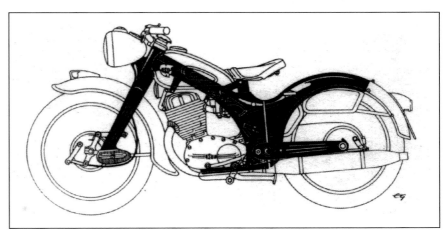

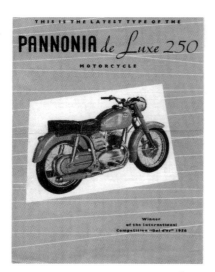

The 247cc Pannonia two-stroke from Hungary made a flitting appearance at an Earls Court Show, and then disappeared from the UK market almost as quickly. It closely resembled the Jawa and was produced in the Csepel armaments factory in Budapest.

marques were achieving prominence as a result of competition success, particularly in events of international status. They had won the Silver Vase trophy in the 1955 ISDT and capitalised on it by displaying one of the actual winning 148cc models on the stand. Also on offer were the, by now familiar, three standard road-going models, the 148cc Junior and 248cc Favorit two-stroke singles and the 344cc Senior two-stroke twin, both unquestionably good value for money at that time.

Making a first appearance in Britain, but not seen at the show, was Adler, the German manufacturer better known in this country for its typewriters and other office equipment. Through Avon Autos of 165, Uxbridge Road, London W7, the company's UK Concessionaire, on display were the MB250 247cc twin cylinder two-stroke of typical Continental styling and also a scooter. The MB250, which retailed at £213, must have made quite an impression on Ariel's designer, Val Page as, when his Ariel Leader was launched in July 1958, it bore marked similarities.

Another absentee from the show but new to Britain for the first time since the war was DKW, the foremost of the German two-stroke manufacturers. Available through AFN Limited of Isleworth, Middlesex (also the BMW and Steib sidecar importer) was the RT 350 model and a scooter with automatic transmission. The RT350, a twin cylinder two-stroke, was a quality product as expected - at a price. At £290.3s.3d it cost about £80 more than a 350cc AJS or Matchless at that time, and almost £200 more than the 344cc Jawa twin. This did not bode well for sales prospects in Britain, apart from a few sold to two-stroke twin fanatics. Not many were sold and imports ceased during October 1957.

TWN continued to stay away from the show but could again offer its range of four motorcycles, little changed in specification. This it did through dealers who sold cheap, discounted bikes. Pride and Clarke sold the Cornet, which other dealers would not service.

The British motorcycle industry faced a dilemma. With imports now almost equalling exports, other questions needed to be answered and it was still not known to what extent moped riders would eventually transfer to a larger capacity motorcycle although, in all probability, the number was relatively small and of no immediate concern. Yet, on the other hand, as mentioned earlier, there seemed an unawareness of the value of brand loyalty and the affect it would have on those who did make the change. This would become of increasing importance in the years ahead.

Scooters continued to provide good business and attracted their own type of user. One burning question needed to be answered: how was it so many foreign-made scooters were being imported and sold at a price that compared favourably with that of the British-made scooters, despite the fact that import duty had been included in the purchase price?

Looking at the larger capacity motorcycles, the British twins were becoming stereotyped, falling neatly into 500s or 650s with a basic similarity. Sidecar drivers had a more restricted choice and some still hankered for a large capacity British vee twin that no longer existed. British design was beginning to stagnate into little more than badge engineering. There was still a reluctance amongst British manufacturers to acknowledge the existence of shaft drive, whilst even the final drive chain was given nothing like adequate protection by the majority, let alone full enclosure. Only recently had manufacturers acknowledged a shortage of 250cc four strokes and made attempts to redress the situation. As usual, the industry was slow to react; it was as though it acknowledged its own shortcomings but was not prepared to do much about them!

Surprisingly, a decision had been made to hold the Motor Cycle Show only in alternate years after 1956 as it was felt the industry would have relatively little to offer that was new every year! There was also discussion about why it was always held at Earls Court in London and pressure was applied to stage it in a number of provincial cities and towns in densely populated areas that had an adequate exhibition hall. It took some time for this to happen, though, as it was not until 1963 that the show was held in Blackpool.

The balance between imports and exports improved a trifle in 1956 with imports down by just over 11,000 and exports down by about 2000, the respective figures being 48,200 and 58,800. At least part of the reason for this was the Middle East crisis that created petrol shortages during the second half of the year and resulted in the re-introduction of petrol rationing by mid-December.

The German and Italian manufacturers were now consolidating their profitable foothold in the UK marketplace. Most had already achieved part of their objective by initially exporting scooters and/or mopeds to the UK a year or two earlier, which had given them a firm financial base on which to build sales. Ducati and Puch had already done so, whilst NSU and Zundapp pioneered a different route by having an established British manufacturer act as their UK distributor.

Now Maico, Maserati and MV Agusta were poised to enter the UK market, mostly with larger capacity models that quickly dispelled the belief that foreign competition could be expected from small capacity models only.

At the 1956 show, BMW continued to display the well-known quartet of four; a single and three twins. Although DKW now had a stand at Earls Court, its display was restricted to Hobby scooters. Jawa-CZ had two new lightweight singles of 125cc and 175cc capacity, both single cylinder two-strokes, as well as the well-proven 248cc Favorit and 344cc Senior models. The former continued to sell well for a long time.

Maico - who had shown up well in the International Six Days Trial - launched the very stylish twin cylinder 350cc and 397cc Taifuns which had created quite an impression at the earlier Frankfurt Show, as well as the 248cc Blizzard roadster and its Scrambler counterpart. Represented by Maico (Great Britain) Limited of 23, Astwood Mews, Courtfield Road, London SW7, the 397cc Taifun was listed at £291 but no price was available for its lower capacity sister. The 248cc Blizzard was priced at £228.9s. and the Scrambler at £248. All were powered by two-stroke engines.

Maserati, the famous Italian car manufacturer, sprang a surprise by showing three models: the 125/TV22

Maserati unexpectedly displayed a range of three motorcycles at the 1956 Motor Cycle Show, comprising a two-stroke and two ohv singles. As may be expected, they were made to the high standards set by this Italian prestige car manufacturer but were highly priced, too, the 250cc/T4 model retailing at £306. Effectively, Maserati priced the machines out of the UK market, although this fact caused the company little concern as it could sell all it could make on the home market.

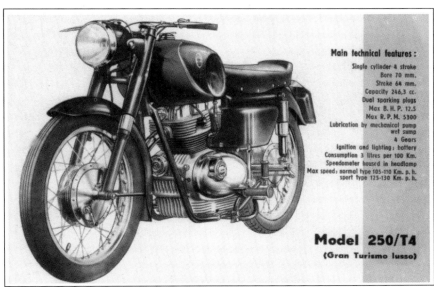

Main technical features :
Single cylinder 4 stroke
Bore 70 mm.
Stroke 64 mm.
Capacity 246,3 cc.
Dual sparking plugs
Max B.H.P. 12.5
Max R.P.M. 5300
Lubrication by mechanical pump wet sump
4 Gears
Ignition and lighting : battery
Consumption 3 litres per 100 Km.
Speedometer housed in headlamp
Max speed: normal type 105-110 Km. p.h.
sport type 125-130 Km. p.h.

Model 250/T4
(Gran Turismo lusso)

Motorcycling in the 50s

Moto Guzzi made a welcome return to the Motor Cycle Show in 1956 with the 235cc unit-construction Lodola. Many found its attractive fire-engine red finish irresistible.

123cc Turismo Veloce, the 160/T4 158cc Turismo Lusso and the 250/T4 246cc Gran Turismo. The Turismo Veloce was a single cylinder two-stroke; the others had a single cylinder ohv engine. Built in a semi-racer style, they were represented by G. Nannucci Limited, of 5-6, Newman Passage, London W1 and prices respectively were £186, £235.12s and

Puch, the Austrian motorcycle manufacturer, specialised in the split single two-stroke type of engine, and could offer two very attractive twin cylinder models operating on the same principle. Note the enclosed carburetter on the SGS250 model.

£308.14s, too high even for a quality product bearing such a reputable name. Maserati got the message and at the next show (in 1958) the motorcycles no longer appeared.

Moto Guzzi had a new model to offer, the 175cc Lodola, powered by a unit-construction single cylinder overhead valve engine, so that company made a welcome return to the show. Also on display were the 98cc Zigolo single cylinder two-stroke and the 73cc Cardellino, as well as a Galetto scooter. Moto Guzzi were now represented in the UK by Motor Imports Co., Ltd. of 7, Gresham Road, London SW9. Price details were not available but the Lodola ended up being sold by Pride and Clarke only, as service and spares - and proper discounts - were not available to the trade at large.

NSU was able to show its latest 247cc Supermax model which mainly differed from the Max by having hydraulically-damped rear suspension units in place of the single spring that previously controlled the pivoted rear fork. It was shown in conjunction with the unchanged 125cc Superfox and a Prima scooter. The cost of the new Supermax? £228.5s to you, sir!

Puch, the Austrian manufacturer famous for its split single two-stroke engine, now showed three motorcycles alongside the two scooters: the road-going 175 SVS and 250 SGS models and the 250 SGSH Scrambler. Already well-established in this country through the range of scooters, the UK concessionaire was Ryder's Autoservices, of 215, Knowsley Road, Bootle, Liverpool 20. The motorcycles created a lot of interest amongst two-stroke enthusiasts; the 175 SVS and the 250 SGS cost £190 and £240 respectively, and the 250 SGSH Scrambler £257.10s.

Zundapp, via Ambassador Motor Cycles Limited, persevered with the 199cc models, the 200S and now the 201S, which differed only in that the latter had an Earles-type front fork. Both were good value at £173.12s.

Ducati did not attend the show, where previously Britax Ltd. had represented the company. Now it was represented by S.D. Sullam Limited of Africa House, Kingsway, London WC2. Still making only small capacity motorcycles, available was the 65T 65cc ohv single and two 98cc ohv singles, the 98T and 98S. These, too, were somewhat expensive at £106.8s.6d for the 65T and £160 and £178.10s respectively for the 98T and 98S models. Behind the scenes, a tug-of-war over importation rights was in progress and many Ducatis were imported without going through Sullams, whose staff knew little about the cut and thrust of the motorcycle trade.

MV Agusta, surprisingly, was not at the show either, despite having a range of five single cylinder models which comprised the 123cc Super Pullman (a single cylinder two-stroke), the 125cc ohv Turismo Rapido, the 172cc ohc Turismo Lusso, the 172cc ohc Modello Sport and the 172cc Super Sport Competizione. As will be seen from the following respective prices, all MV's models tended to be expensive. Like Maserati, MV sold relatively few of them in the UK at £167.8s, £197.3s.3d, £233.2s.5d, £254.4s and £434, the last being a road racing model. The range was now being distributed by M.V. Distributors Limited, of 235-241, Regent Street, London W1.

In 1957 imports rose to an unprecedented level of 115,000 - a ratio of over two to one when compared to British exports over the same period. It is all the more surprising when one considers that petrol rationing as a direct result of the Middle East crisis had not ended until mid-April. There was no show that year due to the new bi-annual ruling and, even if there had been, it was doubtful whether it would have helped to any marked extent. With both

Motorcycling in the 50s

The German-made 345cc Victoria Bergmeister 80 degree ohv vee-twin was unusual in many respects, not the least being the use of duplex chains in its gearbox in place of the usual pinions. Few were sold in the UK; this example is on display in the Sammy Miller Museum.

Italy and Germany having made serious inroads into the British home market, the writing was on the wall. Some dealers began to consider relinquishing all their dealerships in order to diversify into selling cars. Some were already heavily into scooters and bubblecars now that motorcycle insurance costs were rocketing as a result of the boom years having pushed up accident levels and claims.

During the year, Adler introduced two more models and also updated the basic model (now known as the Favorit) by supplying it with pivoted fork rear suspension controlled by hydraulically-damped suspension units, and wheels with full-width hubs. The new models were the Sprinter, a Favorit fitted with a higher performance engine, and a Moto Cross model, neither of which sold at all well.

BMW had now replaced the R25/3 single with the new R26 model which had a higher compression ratio engine and pivoted fork rear suspension. Also available was a 590cc R60 twin, the touring version of the R69.

Ducati ventured further into larger capacity models by offering the 175S Sports model, a 174cc ohc single. Gilera which shared the same importer as Moto Guzzi - Motor Imports Co., Ltd. - and brought in the 173cc ohv single, later known as the 175 Sports model.

Victoria, one of the lesser-known German manufacturers which had been importing scooters, introduced the 197cc single cylinder two-stroke known as the Swing. It had an unusual feature; a electro-magnetically operated four-speed gearbox.

Fewer foreign machines were imported in 1958 as the market became saturated, the figure dropping back to 75,500. British exports fell back, too, to a total of only 36,700, meaning the adverse ratio of two to one still persisted. Yet another Italian manufacturer, Itom, exhibited at the end of the year Motor Cycle Show, displaying the Tabor Sports model, a 65cc single cylinder two-stroke. It cost £117.9s.6d and could be supplied by Adimar of 61, Clapham Road, London SW9. Montesa reappeared, represented by Montesa Motor Cycles (GB) of 42, St. Albans Road, Watford, Herts., who sold the Brio 110 model, a 124cc single cylinder two-stroke, for £178.

Although not at the show, Fred Warr, the London-based long-time Harley-Davidson enthusiast and dealer, could offer three 883cc ohv big twins: the XL Sportster, the XLH Sportster and the XLCH Competition. For those who wanted even more 'cubes', there were two massive 1213cc ohv twins: the FL and the FLHF Duo-Glide. Fred's Fulham Road premises were a haven of Americana and he had the whole market to himself.

At the other end of the scale was the ST165 single cylinder two-stroke, HD's own interpretation of the original DKW RT125 which had formed the basis of the BSA Bantam. America, too, had acquired DKW's original design drawings as the result of war reparation. All the models were expensive, although it is difficult to make direct comparisons as vee twins were no longer

made in Britain. The 883cc twins cost £629.7s., £642.2s.6d. and £685.4s. respectively, whilst the 1213cc twins, with their luxury specifications, were even more expensive, naturally enough, at £680.3s. and £713.0s.8d. Even the ST165 cost £262.9s.; only £5 less than a Triumph Tiger 100! The small following of enthusiasts at that time was nothing like that of today!

Show-goers rejoiced at an announcement made just two months before the show opened. The government had decided to relax restrictions on credit sales so that deposits could be lowered and repayments made over a longer period. It had an instant affect as the following month saw credit sales increase from 5822 to 8201. The sale of secondhand machines rose even more during the same month by just under 6000. 1959 was clearly going to be another record year by a handsome margin. The scene moved from bust to boom as governments all around the world battled with inflation and the demand for higher wages and more consumer goods.

The prediction was accurate, although increased sales at a new high of 173,000 were more in favour of imports. Unfortunately, exports fell far behind, increasing the ratio of imports to exports to three to one. It was not the kind of news the British motorcycle industry expected to hear for it highlighted the increasing tendency to 'buy foreign' because there was so little by way of British manufacture.

There was no Motor Cycle Show in 1959 either, as the bi-annual plan still held good. It did not, however, prevent two more Continental manufacturers from entering the UK market, and one who was already importing scooters to include motorcycles.

Towards the end of the year, Capriolo from Italy seized the opportunity to introduce its 75TV model, a 75cc ohc single cylinder model. It was available from Capriolo Ltd. of 66-68, Southbridge Road, Croydon, Surrey and cost £123. Despite its small engine capacity, it attracted a good deal of attention: styled in typical Italian fashion to give the appearance of a mini-racer, it had the performance to match.

Cimatti came into the UK market too, also from Italy and at about the same time, with a 75cc single cylinder two-stroke, the Model 75. It was imported for only four months, accompanied by a larger capacity 124cc ohv single, the Model 125. Cimatti's venture was short-lived as four months later imports of both models were discontinued.

Parilla must have had the most inappropriately named motorcycle of all time: during November it introduced the 98cc ohv single cylinder Slughi model. It was distributed by Moto Parilla Concessionaires of Bromsgrove, Worcs., who was already importing Parilla scooters. The Slughi retailed at £156.16s.3d. and was superseded a year later by the more suitably named Olimpia 99 model, which differed in many respects to its predecessor.

DKW had by now dropped the earlier RT350 model, replacing it with the smaller capacity RT200VS single cylinder two-stroke in September 1958. This was another machine that created quite an impact and looked as though it might challenge the Zundapp 200S and 201S models, had it not been withdrawn after only five months. A smaller capacity version, the 174cc RT175 model, was imported for an even shorter period - just one month - before it, too, suffered a similar fate.

Ducati Concessionaires had begun a successful breakthrough, capacity-wise, as early in the year imports of the 204cc ohc models, the Elite and the 200 Super Sports, commenced. They were priced at £269.17s.3d. and

Motorcycling in the 50s

DKW RT 175 VS

DKW RT 250 VS

Two-stroke enthusiasts always had great respect for the DKW name but price tended to limit sales more to the smaller capacity RT175 and RT250 single cylinder models. You had to be a two-stroke enthusiast to really appreciate one!

£274.4s.7d, respectively. Neither model remained in production for long, a situation later repeated with other Ducati models. This created endless problems with spare parts.

All importers rejoiced at the news that, by the end of the year, imports hit the even higher level of 173,000. Whilst the British manufacturers managed to improve a little, the number of exports had increased by only a modest 6000. The ratio of imports to exports had risen again to four to one.

The production of motorcycles by British manufacturers increased from 171,300 in 1950 to 234,300 in 1959, which, on paper, looked good. It was the highest annual figure the industry had ever recorded, way above that recorded during the so-called 'golden years of motorcycling' in the mid to late twenties. Yet sadly, it marked the beginning of the industry's terminal decline. From 1960 on, production began to fall steadily, to virtually 50% of this level by the end of the next decade. The import figure wavered throughout the sixties, from a high of 186,200 in 1964 to a low of 48,700 in 1966. Exports also wavered, but not to such a marked extent, falling to 29,000 in 1962 and rising to 60,000 in 1966. The good days were over.

It has been said that statistics can be made to prove anything and, as can be seen from the foregoing figures, there was nothing in them that showed the British motorcycle industry was heading towards oblivion. Nails were hammered into the coffin when Honda made its debut at the 1960 Motor Cycle Show. Yamaha was there in 1962 and Suzuki in 1964.

Siting of the UK establishment of Suzuki was particularly ironic as that company occupied the rear of the James factory in Greet, Birmingham, which was owned by Associated Motor Cycles Ltd. who had taken Suzuki under its wing. Not so long before, one of AMC's directors had claimed motorcyclists loved to spend a Sunday morning taking off their bike's cylinder head and re-seating the valves. He also believed the scooter was no more than a passing fad! Pronouncements such as these (and there were many of them) showed how so many of the captains of the British motorcycle industry were completely out of touch with the change in customer requirements, brought about by the foreign 'invasion'. By the time they decided to try and fight back, it was, as usual, far too late ...

An affection for old bikes

Before World War 2 there was little interest in old motorcycles, which were generally regarded as worthless if more than a decade or so old. With luck, a dealer might be persuaded to accept one in part-exchange for a small trade-in allowance, if a new, or relatively new, secondhand machine was being purchased. Otherwise it was a case of selling it to a scrap dealer or pushing it to the back of a garage or shed where it would deteriorate slowly as a result of neglect. Many motorcycles suffered an even worse fate, pushed out into the garden and abandoned under a sheet of corrugated iron, or covered by sacks, to deteriorate even more rapidly. Some were used to block a hole in a hedge, or even buried amongst the hard core when concrete was laid.

Against these odds, however, quite a few survived, only for some to be destroyed in air raids during the war, along with their owner's property and often the owner. Others, after some heart-searching, were donated by patriotic owners to aid the nationwide scrap metal drive and help the war effort. Those that did remain rarely took to the road again. A thoughtful few, with cherished memories of peacetime days, might have kept them clean and turned the engine over from time to time, but that was all.

There were, of course, museums where old motorcycles could be seen on display, especially the Science Museum in London and its counterparts in Birmingham and Coventry, the hub of the British motorcycle industry. In the early days, Gamages store in Holborn had its own private museum of cars and motorcycles. There were private collections, too, amongst them one owned by Rex Judd, a one-time very successful Brooklands racer who ran a motorcycle dealership in Edgware, Middlesex.

It was the Sunbeam MCC, in conjunction with the Association of Pioneer Motor Cyclists, that played an early leading role in recognising the value of old motorcycles and the need to preserve them. On 9th February 1930, the Sunbeam MCC organised a Pioneer Run for machines manufactured before 31st December 1914. Starting at Croydon Aerodrome and finishing at The Pylons,

Motorcycling in the 50s

Programme - Price 2d.

THE
PIONEER RUN
FOR MOTOR CYCLES OF HISTORIC INTEREST
—9th FEBRUARY, 1930—

Promoted by the Sunbeam Motor Cycle Club in conjunction with the Association of Pioneer Motorcyclists

MOTOR CYCLING

★ The Journal with the Green Cover - Wednesdays 3d.

EVERY keen motorcyclist takes "Motor Cycling" every week. He knows that "Motor Cycling" will give him vital facts and information that will enable him to get the utmost out of his machine.

He knows that "Motor Cycling" is first out with all the news, and that in short, he simply cannot afford to miss a single issue.

"Motorcycling Manual" ALL about motorcycles, and the art of driving them. This manual covers the whole subject and is an indispensable guide for both beginner and expert.

Price 2/6 net. Of all booksellers and bookstalls.

TEMPLE PRESS LTD., 3-15, ROSEBERRY AVENUE, LONDON, E.C.1.

Front cover of the programme for the first Sunbeam MCC Pioneer Run (1930), above, and, below, a diagram of the route and approximate times of arrival.

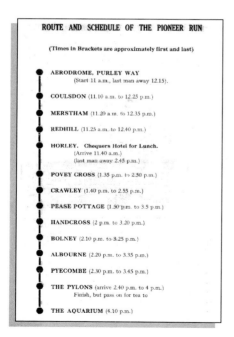

ROUTE AND SCHEDULE OF THE PIONEER RUN

(Times in Brackets are approximately first and last)

- **AERODROME, PURLEY WAY** (Start 11 a.m., last man away 12.15).
- **COULSDON** (11.10 a.m. to 12.25 p.m.)
- **MERSTHAM** (11.20 a.m. to 12.35 p.m.)
- **REDHILL** (11.25 a.m. to 12.40 p.m.)
- **HORLEY. Chequers Hotel for Lunch.** (Arrive 11.40 a.m.) (last man away 2.45 p.m.)
- **POVEY CROSS** (1.35 p.m. to 2.50 p.m.)
- **CRAWLEY** (1.40 p.m. to 2.55 p.m.)
- **PEASE POTTAGE** (1.50 p.m. to 3.5 p.m.)
- **HANDCROSS** (2 p.m. to 3.20 p.m.)
- **BOLNEY** (2.10 p.m. to 3.25 p.m.)
- **ALBOURNE** (2.20 p.m. to 3.35 p.m.)
- **PYECOMBE** (2.30 p.m. to 3.45 p.m.)
- **THE PYLONS** (arrive 2.40 p.m. to 4 p.m.) Finish, but pass on for tea to
- **THE AQUARIUM** (4.10 p.m.)

on the outskirts of Brighton, the run attracted a total of 77 entries and proved such a success that it was continued on an annual basis, with later changes to its route. It is still run today and will be celebrating its 60th anniversary in 1997. Interestingly, the original definition of a veteran motorcycle as being one made before 31st December 1914 still holds good today.

After war had been declared on 3rd September 1939, the two motorcycling weeklies were hard put to find sufficiently interesting copy to retain their respective readerships, let alone the paper to print it on. It was Captain J.J. Hall who triggered off an interest in old motorcycles when he began writing about them in *Motor Cycling*. He started with an article entitled *I Remember ...* in the 21st February 1941 issue, based on his earlier experiences at Brooklands. This and two follow-up articles led to a spate of correspondence about old motorcycles in the magazine's correspondence columns, enough so that a reader who signed himself N.R.T. was moved to ask "Why not a vintage club?"

Captain Hall responded with yet another article in the 28th August issue, entitled *The Gentle Art of Collecting Ancient Motorcycles*. He was unearthing them all over the place and buying them for between £2 and £5 a time. He didn't keep them, though, but preferred to pass them on to others and make a small profit. He found enough to keep his articles about these discoveries going for some considerable time, fostering an ever-widening interest in these machines of yesteryear. Correspondence from readers about them continued, including a letter from one C.E. (Titch) Allen, who was then serving in the army. It was his enthusiasm that led to the holding of an inaugural meeting of old bike enthusiasts at the Lounge Cafe, on the Hogs Back, near Guildford, Surrey. About 40 enthusiasts turned out on Sunday 28th April 1946 and, as a

'Titch' Allen and his wife, Jess, on their return from the 1953 Monte Carlo Rally. They travelled over the Alps from Oxford to Monte Carlo, against the clock and without sleep or a proper meal. "The toughest ride of my life" says Titch, "The 600cc Panther engine was magnificent; the rest of the bike less so." Of 139 starters, Titch finished 91st out of the 98 finishers! (Courtesy C.E. Allen)

result, the Vintage Motor Cycle Club was formed. Appropriately, Captain J.J. Hall was elected its first President.

Until then there had been little evidence of any desire to restore to 'as new' condition an old motorcycle taken out of retirement or rescued from a derelict outhouse after years of neglect. It mattered not that a more modern carburetter or magneto may have been fitted to replace the worn out originals, or later parts substituted for minor components that had gone astray. The main essential was to get the machine running again, without having to spend time restoring faded or damaged paintwork, or peeling

H.O. Twitchen's last but one restoration, a 1919 Model H Triumph. In two respects only it differed from the original in order that it could be safely used on the roads; it had a modern speedometer and wired-on tyres of the original size and section.

nickel plating. No wonder, therefore, that the words 'old crock' were used only too frequently in newspaper reports about old bike events, because that is how spectators saw them.

One man thought it about time to change all this and bring about an air of respectability, not only to the old bikes, but to their riders and the clubs that organised events for them. H.O. (Twitch) Twitchen, a civil servant working for the Ministry of Supply, had been transferred to Southport for the duration of the war. With a knowledge like no other of old Triumph motorcycles, he restored to 'as new' condition a vintage Junior (Baby) Triumph two-stroke, which he gave to Captain Hall in 1941. Working in rented accommodation, and with limited facilities, he then set about the restoration of a Model P Triumph, which subsequently formed the basis of a feature in one of the wartime issues of *Motor Cycling*. He and his wife had come across it when taking an evening stroll across a field, where it had been buried with only its handlebars showing above the ground! This, too, ended up as though it had just left the old Triumph factory in Coventry. The standard of restoration dumfounded Graham Walker, the editor of the magazine, to such an extent that he coined the phrase 'to Twitchenise a bike'. Neither restoration had been easy, especially in wartime, as not only was work of this nature unknown, but also few could understand why anyone should wish to restore an old relic to such an exceptionally high standard!

The Ministry of Supply returned to London after the war and 'Twitch' to his native Kingston-on-Thames. Soon after becoming a member of the Sunbeam MCC's Pioneer Sub-Committee, he put forward some recommendations aimed at raising the standard of machines taking part in the annual Pioneer Run. They amounted to ensuring every machine had to have its details recorded in the Pioneer Machine Register before it could participate in the Run, and have a valid Pioneer Machine Certificate. It also meant that, henceforth, photographs of a machine provided by an applicant would be more closely scrutinised to ensure the machine was as near as possible to its manufacturer's original specification before a Certificate was issued. An additional recommendation was that if a machine had been restored to a very high standard, or had been kept in such a condition, it be awarded a Special Pioneer Machine Certificate in recognition of this.

Motorcycling in the 50s

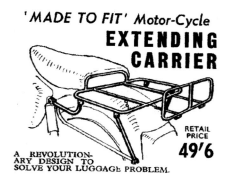

'MADE TO FIT' Motor-Cycle
EXTENDING CARRIER

RETAIL
PRICE
49'6

A REVOLUTION-
ARY DESIGN TO
SOLVE YOUR LUGGAGE PROBLEM.

His recommendations were accepted and implemented in the main. Within a few years, the appearance of the machines taking part in the Run had improved dramatically and no longer were the less well-informed members of the press able to refer to them as 'old crocks'.

Understandably, the award of a Special Pioneer Machine Certificate proved difficult to uphold, without subjecting each machine to close scrutiny by an expert. Photographs supplied by an owner could prove deceptive, as soon became apparent. It had been a good idea in theory but one almost impossible to implement, so eventually it was dropped.

The newly-formed Vintage MCC accepted without hesitation the Sunbeam MCC's veteran machine cut-off date of 31st December 1914, and fixed its own cut-off date for vintage machines at 31st December 1930. This defined two distinct categories of machine, veteran and vintage, a common sense segregation that still holds good today. Some may find it difficult to believe that when the Vintage MCC's deadline was set up, a *bona fide* vintage motorcycle as little as 16 years old would qualify!

For a good many years to come, a machine eligible to take part in Vintage MCC events had to comply with the fixed deadline, although this had to be relaxed much later to take in machines of more recent manufacture which would otherwise have been lost altogether. With a great deal of heart-searching and no small amount of debate, a minimum 25 year old cut-off date was substituted which, even today, remains a contentious issue. The clearly defined vintage date span remains, however, preserved by the addition of more pre-determined classes to cater for the inclusion of the more modern machines. As 'Titch' Allen himself has observed more than once, you can't turn the clock back.

The early activities of the Vintage MCC were mainly localised events of a sporting nature, such as hillclimbs and sprints, although there were also rallies of one kind or another to cater for the rider who had no sporting ambitions. It soon became evident, however, that the club needed a prestige event of its own, along the lines of the Sunbeam MCC's Pioneer Run. Ivor Mutton, one of the leading lights in the Redditch area, came up with the idea of running such an event in the Midlands, to take in some of the roads (and hills) the works testers would have used in the early days. As a direct result, the Vintage MCC staged its first 42 mile Reliability Run from Birmingham to Banbury on 26th June 1949. It attracted an entry of 80 and took in the 1 in 7 Edge Hill, finishing in Banbury's historic Horse Fair with the result that thereafter the Run, now into its 46th year, took that town's name in its title.

The racing fraternity managed to get a vintage machine race included in *Motor Cycling's* Silverstone Saturday programme the following year, which again helped the Club gain additional publicity. By the beginning of 1953 when the Club published for the first time its magazine in a properly printed format, it boasted 400 members. To simplify administration, the Club by now had been sub-divided into the Southern, Midland and Northern Regions and, in the fullness of time, these regions were further sub-divided into a number of Sections. Each of these Sections was based on areas where there was evidence of a high level of enthusiasm and identified by the county. By January 1956 the membership level had risen to 600 and, by the end of 1959, to over 1000.

As the level of interest in old motorcycles began to grow, it was inevitable the machines would increase in value. By the end of the decade it was no

Right: Butterflies! The author waits to be called to the grid in his first ever road race at Goodwood in 1951. His machine is a 1927 Model 18 Norton, on which he finished 10th in the Vintage Race. His mechanic, Alan Swan, wears an ex-WD combat jacket. Heavy rain (and hail) on practice day the day before had turned the paddock area into a quagmire.

longer possible to buy an old machine in running order for around the £5-£10 mark. A threefold increase had by now become the norm for anything that could be considered worth buying. The upward spiral had begun, which accelerated after the Beaulieu Motor Museum held its first auction of historic vehicles in 1960. The re-

Below: On the grid before the start, worries are replaced by keen anticipation. There is a good selection of pre-1931 vintage machines including Norton, Scott, Rex Acme, AJS and Ariel. This proved to be the only road race meeting for motorcycles held at this West Sussex track.

Motorcycling in the 50s

Sprinting also received much support from Vintage MCC members. Having changed allegiance to a 1927 348cc KSS Velocette, the author lifts off at the start of a Sunbeam MCC Sprint at Aldershot in October 1954. The machine was bought locally in Crawley, West Sussex and prepared for racing.

sultant publicity made the general public much more aware of the historic value of these machines.

By now, another club with an interest in old motorcycles had emerged, the Collectors' Club, with which both Joe Greer and Percy Clare were much involved. It was aimed at those who owned old machines but did not necessarily wish to ride them, perceiving them more as static objects of desire. Meetings were held in the vicinity of London's Euston Station, the membership comprising a large number of those who were also members of the Sunbeam and Vintage MCCs. It was through Joe Greer that Lord Montagu came to accept Beaulieu as a venue for old motorcycle gatherings - and to include old motorcycles in his Motor Museum, some of them on loan from club members. When he retired as editor of *Motor Cycling* Graham Walker went to Beaulieu Museum as its Curator.

Until 1950, the Vintage MCC's *Bulletin* had been the only publication to cover exclusively the interests of old motorcycle enthusiasts, although news items about them were still appearing on a regular basis in the two motorcycling weeklies. When *Motor Cycle News* appeared on the scene on 30th November 1955, that, too, showed an interest in machines of the past, as did Lord Montagu's *Vintage and Veteran Magazine*, a monthly publication launched during August of the following year. Other new magazines catering solely for old motorcycles followed as, by, now there could be few motorcyclists who did not show some kind of an interest in the past. Books about the subject were, however, few and far between. Apart from Ixion's *Motor Cycle Cavalcade* mentioned earlier and published in 1950, it was not until 1961 that the first substantial work appeared, Jim Sheldon's *Veteran and Vintage Motor Cycles* published by Batsford.

Over forty years on, the old motorcycle scene has changed almost beyond recognition. The Vintage MCC now boasts over 12,000 members, world-wide, whilst the majority of the larger capacity motorcycles more than 25 years old change hands for four figure sums. Some of the more exotic machines, such as the Brough-Superior SS100, have realised as much as £25,000! There is now a National Motorcycle Museum, too, where British bikes only are seen, adjacent to the M42 and close to the National Exhibition Centre. Only someone with the drive and determination of its founder, Roy Richards, could have seen such an ambitious project through to its conclusion.

Restoration has become the 'in' thing, with many machines rebuilt to a standard that would astound even 'Twitch' by their quality and depth of attention to detail. A host of replacement parts for machines long out of production is being made, and there are classic bike shows and autojumbles held all over the country on most weekends of the year. Classic motorcycle magazines and newspapers abound, and there are so many books and manuals on the market that the choice is almost infinite. As for events, although the Pioneer Run and the Banbury Run remain highlights in the veteran and vintage motorcyclist's calendar, there are so many others being run during the 'riding season' it is virtually impossible to avoid confliction.

The restoration of old motorcycles is by no means restricted to the UK. Enthusiasm in America is now approaching hitherto unseen levels, whilst on the Continent there is increasing appeal for British riders to take part in cross-Channel events and vice-versa. It is by no means uncommon to hear foreign languages spoken at some of the larger autojumbles and shows, such as those held at Beaulieu and Stafford.

Although the UK motorcycle mar-

L.P. Peters of Coulsdon, who owned this 1924 Brough Superior and sidecar from new, would have been astounded if he had known how highly it would be valued in the late 1980s. The outfit may well have topped the £20,000 mark!

Old motorcycles still crop up unexpectedly after having lain dormant for years. Sammy Miller discovered this one-owner-from-new 1908 Triumph only a matter of miles from his museum. A big question then arose - should it be restored or made to run as it was and retain the patina of age? One thing is certain; its front tyre will cause it to fail an MoT test!

This 1924 totally original 'big port' AJS was found in Somerset a few years ago, when only a lack of sparks from the magneto prevented it from being started. It was last licensed in 1930, as the photo of the tax disc confirms.

ket has gone downhill dramatically since it last recorded a 'high' in 1980, the interest in old machines has remained buoyant and, if anything, has continued to grow. Even though it represents only a small sector of the overall market, could 'Titch' Allen ever have foreseen when he founded the Vintage MCC way back in 1946 that the revival of interest in old bikes would reach anything like today's level?

A lucky find for someone! A somewhat rare but complete 1926 overhead camshaft Velocette first registered in Dorset. Every vintage enthusiast dreams of finding a bike in this condition, which makes restoration relatively easy as there are no missing parts to locate.

Motorcycling gets a bad name

Today, the media pays a great deal of attention to vehicle-related crime and not without good reason. Any vehicle that has been parked unattended and is not under close vigilance, is at risk, the more so if it is of the exotic or high performance type. Some are stolen 'to order' and never seen again, their identity changed out of all recognition. Others are stripped down and parts used to rejuvenate what were insurance write-offs, to be sold to unsuspecting customers. Some are taken by 'joy riders' to show off their dubious skills in handling to whoever happens to witness their impromptu back street displays. Inevitably, the display ends when the vehicle is either crashed and written-off, or abandoned, set on fire and burnt out. There has been such an high incidence of this type of crime in recent years that many have come to regard it as an inevitable part of today's way of life. Yet is this undesirable trend really new, or have we forgotten what things were like some forty or so years ago?

In 1950, an outbreak of lawlessness throughout Britain was causing a great deal of concern. The previous year in the London Metropolitan Police area more than 1000 motorcycles had been stolen or, to put it in police parlance, 'driven away without the owner's consent'. Although reference was made to 'joy riding', it had a different connotation then. Often, a motorcycle was stolen to save the thief a long walk from A to B, after the last bus had been missed. Statistics - which showed that out of the 1000 motorcycles stolen, 750 were subsequently recovered - seemed to confirm this, although some were found on recovery to be damaged or with parts removed. There was no real answer to the problem then, any more than there is now, except to make a motorcycle more difficult to steal by immobilising it so that it could not be wheeled to a waiting van and ensuring that insurance cover included loss by theft: third party cover or Road Traffic Act alone was clearly inadequate. In the fifties, of course, the policeman on his beat was much more in evidence, as were random checks carried out on traffic late at night.

Noise was a constant cause for complaint. To quote one example, the Par-

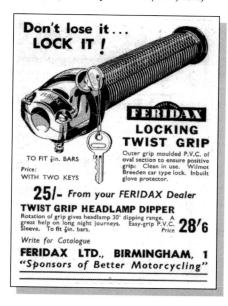

Feridax produced a locking twist grip to help reduce motorcycle thefts. It had one disadvantage; it would only lock when the twist grip was in the wide open position, placing an unnecessary strain on the cable and throttle valve return spring and, unless an air filter was fitted, anything could drop into the cylinder head. (Courtesy Feridax (1957) Ltd)

Motorcycling in the 50s

ish Council of Basildon requested that the Bradfield Rural District Council and Chief Constable of Berkshire do something about reducing the noise of the 'hundreds of motorcycles' that passed through Basildon *en route* to a weekend scramble. It was no more than a storm in a teacup, however, stirred up by a prejudiced and selfish community. A subsequent investigation showed there were only three scrambles a year held at the venue mentioned! Even so, road behaviour was far from exemplary, especially on the A20 in the vicinity of Brands Hatch with fast motorcyclists showing off on their way to, and returning from, the meetings. Ironically, motorcycle sport enjoyed an enthusiastic following from the general public: over 40,000 attended the 1950 Silverstone Saturday meeting and a similar number turned up when Blandford held the first international road race meeting that year.

As far as off-road events - especially trials - were concerned, few seemed over-concerned about the effect these events were having on the environment. When a rural district council employee had cause to write to the motorcycle press about damage to footpaths in his area, it prompted Ralph Venables to respond and highlight what was becoming a major issue. As well as being a leading motorcycle journalist and events organiser, Ralph respected the countryside and so emphasised how important it was that organisers of trials should take more care how, and where, they planned their routes. He recommended that the issue of an A-CU permit should at the discretion of local councils and the police. Well aware of the growing alarm about the way in which trials riding was inflicting unnecessary damage on the countryside, he knew that, already, many ancient rights of way had begun to disappear, or have their use restricted by the appearance of 'Closed to Motors' notices. It was time to take action and forestall an issue that otherwise would become even more contentious in future years.

An additional problem arose after the ending of petrol rationing. With the resumption of long distance reliability trials, there was now the possibility of large numbers of motorcyclists disturbing residents during the night as they passed through towns, villages and even country lanes. It was suggested by the motorcycling press that the A-CU would be wise to pay special attention to this problem and issue permits for such events somewhat guardedly. Eventually, the RAC took charge of all road events on a strictly rationed and route consultation basis.

Road accidents had always been an emotive subject yet, strangely enough, the question of head injuries, to which the motorcyclist is particularly prone, received little attention. In July 1950 during a debate on road safety in the House of Lords, Lord Llewellin, President of the Royal Society for the Prevention of Accidents, disclosed that an analysis of 146,000 accidents had shown pedestrians were responsible for 28% of them, car drivers 25%, passengers 9%, cyclists 17% and motorcyclists 8%, the remainder being attributable to a variety of miscellaneous causes including lorries. Lord Lucas, the Parliamentary Secretary to the Minister of Transport, hinted that restrictive measures may have to be adopted if this seemed the only way in which to help resolve a growing problem.

Although nothing had been said to this effect, the motorcycling press interpreted Lord Lucas's remarks as a hint that the compulsory wearing of safety helmets was being seen as an option. It seemed it would be of little consequence to the government if any such legislation infringed the rights of the individual if it helped reduce the number of fatalities and serious injuries. The

Cyclists' Touring Club reacted strongly, resigning from ROSPA forthwith as it believed the Society no longer had its members interests at heart.

To bring matters to a head, Lord Lucas met editorial representatives of the motoring and motorcycling magazines and motoring correspondents of the national press towards the end of the year, in order to debate further the accident problem. Lord Lucas claimed he was 'at his wits' end' to know how to resolve the growing accident problem as 5000 people were killed and 250,000 injured on Britain's roads every year. In his opinion, most accidents were due to carelessness and he expressed concern that the 1939 traffic law and the rudimentary Highway Code were being treated with disrespect. He intended to deploy more mobile police to ensure stronger law enforcement, with harsher penalties for those who showed scant regard for the law, even if it meant suspension of a driving licence.

Directing attention to motorcyclists, Lord Lucas claimed motorcycle accident figures recorded during the period June-August 1950 represented a 56% increase when compared to the corresponding figure in 1949. He went so far as to say that if this trend continued, weight of public opinion would force him to prohibit any motorcycle from exceeding a legally defined speed limit. He considered the motorcycling magazines were to blame by glorifying the exploits of TT and speedway riders! He also openly, for the first time, drew attention to the lack of protective clothing worn by motorcyclists and suggested safety helmets may have to be worn, confirming earlier fears expressed by the motorcycling press.

The media made capital of Lord Lucas's outburst and turned public opinion against motorcyclists. There was only one answer; motorcyclists had now to seize the initiative and be seen to be putting their own house in order. It seemed prudent to recommend that newcomers to motorcycling learn to ride on low-powered machines of 250cc capacity or less, and to encourage all mature riders to wear protective head gear by choice rather than compulsion.

Attempts by the then Minister of Transport, Alfred Barnes, to action the recommendations seemed vague and confused, because he intended to revoke all existing regulations that requested pedestrians to conform to signs at light-controlled road crossings. It would not, however, apply to uncontrolled crossings, where pedestrians would still have precedence over traffic, although he intended reducing these crossings in number. Those that were retained would be made more conspicuous by black and white stripes marking the road surface. Government wheels turn slowly and it took more than a year for these changes to be implemented and zebra crossings to become a reality. Pedestrians could still not be held accountable for causing an accident, and neither were they encouraged to adopt a more responsible attitude.

The TT has always attracted the unwelcome attention of the tabloid 'gutter press', who seized any opportunity to print shock horror stories about the dangers of the 37.75 mile course and the number of riders who had been killed whilst competing in the races. After three riders lost their lives during TT week in 1951, Dr C. Garbett, the Archbishop of York, made his own protestations in a diocesan leaflet. It was not the kind of comment expected from the church ...

Towards the middle of the year it seemed the earlier comments made by Ralph Venables about off-road events had been anything but premature. Most rural district council offices now held maps denoting bridle paths and tracks they intended to downgrade and restrict to vehicular traffic if objections were not filed before a certain deadline by those with a valid reason for opposing closure. Motorcycle club secretaries were urged by the A-CU to inspect these maps and ascertain whether any of the bridle paths or tracks they currently used or had used were likely to be affected. If so, they should lodge an immediate objection. One A-CU centre saw this as such a significant threat it appointed a member who happened to be a specialist in such matters to act on behalf of all of the clubs in that area.

A letter to *The Times* from Sir Hugh Cairns, an eminent surgeon who had made a study of head injuries suffered by army motorcyclists during the war, re-opened the case for the compulsory wearing of safety helmets. Fortunately, the Minister of Transport remained hesitant to recommend any legislation that would result in compulsion, no doubt as the result of having received so many protests, not only from motorcyclists but also the various organisations that represented the interests and civil liberties of motorcyclists. There was also the question of how such legislation could be enforced if it came to be. Most agreed that wearing a helmet made good sense, but consensus of opinion was that it should be a question of choice rather than compulsion.

In the fifties little attention was paid to the condition of Britain's roads, which had suffered years of gross neglect as the result of the war. From the motorcyclist's viewpoint, there were two particular evils: tram lines and wood block road surfaces, both of which were downright dangerous. In many areas where trams had been taken out of service, the lines on which they ran had not been lifted but, instead, were covered by a layer of smooth tar which was not skid-proof and hardened into slippery ridges. As for wood blocks, even if they had been covered by a thin layer of tar, this soon wore off, re-exposing them. A shower of rain was enough to change the surface into the equivalent of a skating rink for the hard rubber tyres of the day. Although motorists and motorcyclists had to purchase a road tax disc, the revenue from which was allegedly used for road maintenance and improvements, only a tiny portion was actually used for this purpose. No-one would deny that many thousands of accidents could be attributed to road conditions, something the government was reluctant to discuss ...

There was also the question of training of learner motorcyclists, many of whom enrolled in the local RAC-ACU Learner Training Scheme. Some local road safety committees appeared unaware of the excellent job being done in their areas by the enthusiastic volunteers who ran these schemes, or that the standard of the RAC-ACU test was much higher than that of the Ministry of Transport driving licence test. Training helped considerably in reducing the accident rate of learner riders by starting them on a 250cc or under lower-powered model, so fulfilling an objective advocated by Lord Lucas.

These and many other problem areas that had now come under the spotlight provoked the government into setting up The Committee on Road Safety, whose brief it was to investigate all accident data and offer whatever recommendations appeared pertinent to help reduce the accident rate. Common sense, it would seem, had prevailed at last.

Before The Committee on Road Safety was able to report its findings, other possibly contributory aspects of the accident problem received attention. The feeble 6 volt rear light on the majority of vehicles (including motorcycles) left much to be desired and British Road Services took the initiative by re-equipping its entire fleet of 40,000 vehicles with twin rear lights and extra reflectors. The Austin Motor Co. Ltd. fell into line with this, ensuring its commercial vehicles were made more visible from the rear at night.

Goaded into action, the Ministry of Transport announced it would be allocating £1,000,000 to road improvements and elimination of danger spots, with local authorities adding a further £500,000. It was also confirmed that the number of mobile police patrols would be increased to ensure those who used the roads developed a greater respect for the law.

When The Committee on Road Safety made its report, the findings were disappointing, amounting to little more than a recommendation that more emphasis be placed on the Highway Code by limiting its content to clear rules of behaviour and separating out the illustrations of traffic signs and signals referred to in these rules to form a separate appendix. The police would then be expected to emphasise any breaches of the Code that had taken place when prosecutions for careless or dangerous driving were brought to court. To reinforce this, it would now be mandatory to declare the Highway Code had been studied when signing the application form for a driving licence. It was here that a big opportunity was missed yet again: although pedestrians and cyclists were just as capable of causing accidents, no provision was made to ensure they were committed to observing the Highway Code, too!

Perhaps surprisingly, the government showed commendable speed in implementing the roads improvement programme, giving priority to the illumination - by flashing beacons - of zebra crossings. Unfortunately, the estimated cost of this, £500,000, accounted for half the amount of money made available. Still far too little was being spent on trying to save lives by preventing accidents.

On the vexed question of safety helmets, one curious anomaly was that although the government was keen to encourage the voluntary wearing of safety helmets the helmets were subject to Purchase Tax (as were miner's helmets!). Pressure was applied to have them made exempt, but it met with strong resistance. Meanwhile, ROPSA was offering a prize of £100 to the motorcycle club who could come up with the best method to popularise the

Lucas ensured motorcycles were provided with better rear lights by using a plastic lens with a built-in reflector to improve the 'fag end' type of illumination provided by the rear lights fitted in the early 50s. Brake-operated stop lights were also a legal necessity unless a machine had no lighting equipment. (Courtesy Lucas Industries plc)

wearing of safety helmets by riders and their pillion passengers.

With everything that would help reduce accidents under close scrutiny, official thought was now given to provisional driving licences. These could still be renewed indefinitely for 5/- (25p) every six months, with no time limit within which a learner rider must pass a driving test.

The inadequacy of the amount of money allocated for road improvements had become a parliamentary and press cause *celebre*. It was acknowledged that road accidents cost £140,000,000 a year and that, collectively, the motoring community contributed more than £300,000,000 a year. Yet, from all the revenue derived from road tax, the government was spending only a miserable 1% on the nation's roadway network. It had not escaped the notice of the press that £250,000 had been allocated for the rebuilding of the Palm House in Kew Gardens!

When Dr H.W. Glanville, the Director of Road Research, read a paper at the Congress of the Institute of Transport in Glasgow, motorcyclists were singled out for comment. Dr Glanville claimed that of 4700 fatalities in road accidents during 1952, 30% of them were the result of motorcycle accidents, either riders or pillion passengers. Calculations showed this represented a cost of £45,000,000, 35% of the cost of all accidents that year. He concluded it would pay the government to fit sidecars to all motorcycles of more than 250cc capacity, free of charge!

When the year's road accident figures were released, the national press made capital of them, provoking further comments from the new (as the result of a change of government) Minister of Transport. John Scott Maclay announced his intention to introduce new regulations that would necessitate all pedal bicycles having two effective brakes, and that he would be spending £845,000 in 1953 on controlled traffic lights at crossroads to ease traffic flow in congested areas. He also said the compulsory wearing of safety helmets by motorcyclists was 'reluctantly' under consideration, as was compulsion by law for pedestrians to use zebra crossings. Other provisions included the issue of a revised edition of the Highway Code mentioned earlier and expenditure of a further £22,000,000 to eliminate accident black spots. There was also talk of an official driving manual and the introduction of special toll roads. The comments from the press and the Minister marked the early beginning of a fresh anti-motorcycling lobby that would gather momentum in later years and single out motorcyclists for the special attention of the legislators. The motorcycling movement had not lobbied or protested in response, so was considered a target that, in respect of safety, could be improved for the good of itself.

Towards the end of the year, a further statement from the Minister of Transport to the House of Commons laid plans for the expenditure of another sum of £50,000,000 on major road improvements within the next three to four years. A step in the right direction, perhaps, but it was still grossly inadequate in relation to the £350,000,000 collected annually from the Road Fund.

Meanwhile, a campaign - initiated by the motorcycling press - to encourage riders and their pillion passengers to wear safety helmets rather than face compulsion was having effect. One helmet manufacturer claimed so many orders had been received that production could not keep pace! Six manufacturers now made helmets to a new British Standard Specification (BS 2001:1953) and some of the road tests conducted by the motorcycling press depicted testers wearing helmets. It was all part of a somewhat patronising (but sensible, in the eyes of many) campaign run along the lines of 'You know it makes sense ...'

1954 proved to be relatively free from further major attempts to discriminate against motorcyclists, although Orpington Urban District Council tried to get a private bill through Parliament to curtail the off-road use of land in its area. Thanks to the vigilance of the South Eastern Centre of the A-CU, a committee of the House of Lords rejected it. Had it gone through 'No company body association or person shall without the permission of the council use any lands or premises in the district for motorcycle trials or scrambles or other similar purposes'. Other councils were poised to follow suit.

At a meeting of The British Association in September, a paper on road safety was read by George Grimes of the Road Research Laboratory. When discussing motorcycle accidents, he touched on another controversial issue by showing that the incidence of severe leg injuries was second only to those sustained to riders' necks and heads. He was of the opinion that only a fully-enclosed three-wheeler was likely to provide the degree of protection necessary to prevent injury. It was a first attempt to voice concern about the need for leg protection but one which was to assume much greater prominence some thirty five or so years later.

One thing motorcyclists did not need at this time was bad publicity. It was therefore all the more disappointing that it should come from an entirely unexpected source. Early in 1955 Marlon Brando's film *The Wild One* was released by the American studio that made it. Initially, the British Board of Film Censors refused to issue a certificate for its showing in Britain as it depicted, in its eyes, the worst kind of anti-social behaviour when a gang of marauding motorcyclists, all on British motorcycles, invaded a small town and terrorised its inhabitants.

By 1954, 18 different safety helmets were on the list approved by the British Standards Institution. All bore the kite mark symbol and conformed to the requirements of British Standard 2001:1953. The Feridax 'St. Christopher' helmet had its own special features and two different kinds were available. Every effort was made to encourage motorcyclists to voluntarily wear a safety helmet rather than make it compulsory to do so. (Courtesy Feridax (1957) Ltd)

Motorcycling in the 50s

Motorcycles were still in widespread use with, sadly, a correspondingly high accident rate that was giving rise to public concern. This is a tiny section of the car park at an early Silverstone Saturday race meeting.

Representative of what had happened in the American town of Hollister, it gave packed cinema audiences the impression that such happenings were likely to become commonplace. When the film was accepted for release in Britain, those who were against motorcycles and would have liked to see them banned made capital of the fear generated by the film. Motorcyclists were now seen by the general public in a different light, even though the fear was never realised, and came to be regarded as potential hooligans, with a total disregard for law and order.

A change in the position of Minister of Transport meant newly-appointed John Boyd-Carpenter quickly got to grips with the vital road building programme. Aware of the gravity of the problem, he proposed spending £212,000,000 to widen trunk roads, provide by-passes around some of the more congested trouble spots and to commission Britain's first motorway. Although the programme would take some years to complete, it was well received and made everyone, including motorcyclists, feel that things would get better.

Publication of the official accident statistics for 1953 proved the value of safety helmets. Although motorcycle accidents had risen to nearly 50,000, the incidence of head injuries had fallen by more than 5%. The report stressed that if all motorcyclists had worn helmets, the number of head injuries would have been halved. The general consensus of opinion was still that all motorcyclists should be encouraged to wear helmets rather than be compelled to by law. The police had already said they would be unable to enforce compulsion if it became the law, whilst to MPs the issue was a real hot potato, when so many of their constituents owned either solos or sidecar outfits. It was an issue that continued to be shelved, even though it re-appeared time and time again. Pressure was mounting gradually for some kind of positive action to be taken and eventually prosperity and greater use of the car would remove the vitally interested but maturing motorcycle enthusiast from the equation. MPs could always legislate against youth!.

A new Road Traffic Act came into effect during late 1956 which finally made pedestrians accountable for their actions. Henceforth, if a pedestrian ignored a traffic control policeman's signals, prosecution could follow. Of benefit to motorcyclists was a requirement to keep a dog on a lead. This was greatly appreciated as stray dogs had been the cause of many accidents. Stiff penalties now awaited anyone - riders or drivers - found guilty of reckless or dangerous driving. Not so good was provision to raise the minimum age for holding a motorcycle driving licence, if required. Also, when a footpath or bridleway was to be used by motorcyclists in off-road events, local authority consent had to be obtained as well as that of the land owner.

Problems with the effectiveness of some safety helmets led to the questioning of the value of British Standard BS 2001:1953. As a result the British

Standards Institution revised its helmet testing procedure to make the quality requirements more stringent. BS 2001:1956 was the outcome, to which a helmet would have to have to conform if statutory requirements eventually became law. Henceforth, it would be illegal to sell an unmarked helmet to the public.

In December 1955, The Committee on Road Safety referred to previously, was requested to reconsider the minimum age limit for riding a motorcycle. That the wheels of officialdom grind slowly became evident when its recommendations were not published until November 1957! Surprisingly, the Committee was in favour of matching European policy by *lowering* the age limit to 15, with the proviso that riding at this age should be restricted to a moped with a maximum speed of 25mph. In addition, it also favoured raising the age limit to 17 for riding machines of over 250cc; these two changes to be interlinked. A further recommendation suggested that a moped rider still be required to take a driving test and that when a full licence was issued it should be restricted to a 50cc moped.

Training was seen as the most sensible way of helping to reduce motorcycle accidents. For several years it had been hoped by the motorcycle industry that after a learner rider had passed the much more demanding RAC/ACU training course, it would be a mere formality to obtain a full driving licence, or even accepted as the qualification. Sadly, any such acceptance was rejected. When, after a further change of office, the new Minister of Transport, Harold Watkinson, looked at the recommendations of The Committee on Road Safety, they, too, were held in abeyance. A marked reluctance to lower the minimum age limit for riding a powered two-wheeler of any kind was always evident. Some of the other recommendations *were* implemented at later dates, however.

The motorcycle-mounted police were already setting a good example by wearing safety helmets, some as early as 1954. This was seen by many as a further step in the right direction helping to encourage the widespread use of helmets by motorcyclists everywhere.

There now occurred discussion about the compulsory official testing for roadworthiness of all vehicles more than ten years old, prior to the granting of a road fund licence. Why this was now regarded as necessary is difficult to understand, because there had been nothing to suggest that old vehicles were more accident prone. Owners of veteran and vintage vehicles were relieved to learn that special concessions would be made in their case because the braking and lighting systems could not be expected to conform to what had become present-day standards. However, these concessions appeared to contradict the reasons for having a test!

An odd ruling was that if, for any reason, a vehicle failed the test, it had to be repaired by the person who had conducted the test, or by another officially recognised tester. Fortunately, this ruling was revised before the test became mandatory, after it had been pointed out that it prevented the vehicle's owner from carrying out his own repairs.

During July 1958 Mr Heathcote Amory, the Chancellor of the Exchequer, finally bowed to pressure and exempted motorcycle safety helmets from Purchase Tax. Why it had taken so long, no-one knew, as there was no logical reason for implementing a tax on safety.

Almost as the year ended, Britain's first motorway was opened by the Prime Minister, Harold Macmillan. Opened with a great amount of hue and

Motorcycling in the 50s

Two RAC motorcycle members are seen here with a Norton Dominator twin, seeking help in finding their way from the once familiar roadside RAC box, whilst the patrolman in the background assists a motorist. The year is 1956 and all are wearing safety helmets. By 1959 it was estimated that 50% of all motorcyclists were wearing a safety helmet voluntarily, which resulted in a measurable drop in serious head injuries. (Courtesy The Royal Automobile Club)

cry, it is doubtful whether it really qualified as a motorway. It was, after all, only a 8.5 mile stretch - the new Preston by-pass! *Cassandra*, the pseudonym of a well-known journalist on the staff of the *Daily Mirror*, took the opportunity to question why motorcycles capable of 120mph could be sold to young lads. This was typical of his frequent sensation-seeking outbursts on all manner of topics so it is doubtful whether many took much notice. Even so, motorcycling could do without such biassed comments from the press at a time when it was coming under the close scrutiny of the government and all those showing concern at the high total number of road accidents. Motorcycles were still accountable for one third of them and the problem seemed unresolvable.

Throughout 1959 motorcyclists were being attacked from yet another quarter. The Noise Abatement Society seized upon the topic that had been all too familiar from the moment the first motorcycles took to the road. Unfortunately, motorcycles had tended to become noisier as their performance range extended, ranging from the flat-sounding staccato note of the Triumph Tiger

Motorcycling gets a bad name

Cub to the high pitched and more ir-ritating noise of a two-stroke. There has always been a tendency for young and less experienced riders to remove baffles from their silencers, under the mistaken impression that more noise gives the impression of greater speed. In point of fact, in nearly every case the end result was quite the reverse, but it attracted the attention to which all young males aspire. It was always possible to design a really effective silencing system that would have little restrictive affect on performance and, in some cases, actually enhance it, especially on two-strokes.

Club runs were always popular, although comparatively few were held during the hours of darkness. The Steyning and District MCC run was an obvious exception, as shown here at Bayards sometime in 1952 before it started. This photograph shows a preference for berets to be worn as headgear, held in place by goggles. Not a safety helmet in sight! (Courtesy Ken Harman)

Surprisingly, Sir Miles Thomas, a well-known personality in the aviation industry, supported the Noise Abatement Society's views and said so during a broadcast. The British Motorcycle Industry Association was quick to respond as he had accused British manufacturers of deliberately making noisy motor-cycles to help boost sales.

Continuing encouragement to wear safety helmets had resulted in them being worn by more than 50% of all motorcyclists on the road, a fact com-mented upon favourably by the Minister of Transport's Parliamentary Secre-tary. There were still some that thought they would be regarded as a 'cissy' if seen wearing one, whilst others were convinced they encouraged a rider 'to play racers'.

November 1959 marked the official opening of Britain's first true motor-way, the M1, which ran from the A41 near Watford to Crick, near Rugby. Sixty six miles long, it cost £20,000,000 to construct. There was no speed limit along its entire length, nor was there any provision for warning traffic of adverse weather conditions, especially fog and ice. A great deal would be learned during the now imminent winter and from those that followed, mostly at the cost of those who suffered serious injury or even lost their lives as a result of motorway accidents.

As time progressed, motorcyclists became the target of more and more adverse attention, even after the wearing of safety helmets had become com-pulsory. The advent of the 'cafe racer' and 'chopper' types of motorcycle only added to the strength of anti-motorcycling comment. Cafe racers were always condemned on account of their often flamboyant riding style, the high level of noise made by the bikes and high accident rate. It was not fully appreciated that they were largely a new breed of modern working class youth trying to establish a new lifestyle for itself.

Later, when the chopper cult appeared and riders took on a generally unkempt appearance, the public re-identified the image with that of the Marlon Brando film and lawlessness in general. Motorcycling had shot itself in the foot and was rapidly becoming its own worst enemy.

Index